CELEBRATE
PEACE

CELEBRATE PEACE
PARTNERS

Peace Cereal

The Peace Company

PEACE X PEACE

Spirit Voyage Music

Utne Magazine

Breathe Magazine

celebratepeace

*108 Simple Ways
to Create a More
Peaceful World*

in your heart

peace

in your world

in your home

in the world

A Special Edition of
The Peace Book

LOUISE DIAMOND

FIRST SPECIAL EDITION

THE PEACE COMPANY
BRISTOL, VERMONT

FIRST SPECIAL EDITION

FIRST PRINTING, JULY 2005

Copyright © 2001, 2005 by Louise Diamond

The Peace Company,
   54 Maple Street, Bristol, Vermont 05443

ISBN: 0-9767982-2-0

Cover Design   Marion Wasserman/Elemental Design

Cover Illustration   Sopurkh Singh

Author Photo   Felice Boucher

Interior Design   Margery Kanter, Winslow Colwell

Printed in Canada on recycled paper

DEDICATION

Celebrating the living spirit of peace
in each and every one of us.

Author's Prologue

FIRST SPECIAL EDITION

Celebrate Peace! What a wonderful idea. In a time of an unending war on terror and rampant violence all around us, what better to celebrate than peace?

What does it mean to celebrate peace? How do you do it? I am reminded of a time many years ago, when I was facilitating a dialogue between Israeli and Palestinian women, and one woman said she was attending the event because she knew 'there had to be a better way.' When I asked her how she knew this, since all her life she and her community had been caught up in endless cycles of violence, fear, sorrow, and revenge, she gently tapped her heart and said, 'Because I just know; I just know.'

The profound truth was in her gesture as much as her words. She was telling us all that in our hearts we have a deep 'knowing' about peace, a profound yearning that compels us to action, even when that action calls us out of our comfort zone or even puts us at risk. I call that inner wisdom 'the living spirit of peace.' I believe we are encoded from birth with this peace seed—it is our spiritual birthright, our soul's DNA—and, like the acorn from the oak tree, it contains all we need to grow to the fullest our potential for peace as a way of life.

Many people challenge my work for peace, saying that violence is inherent in the human condition and that therefore war is inevitable. I believe that this living spirit of peace is also inherent in our being-ness, and our task as the human family in these times is to choose which one we will feed—our capacity for violence or our capacity for peace. The phrase 'celebrate peace' expresses perfectly the choice more and more people are making every day. When enough of us have made this commitment, we will truly change the world.

The pathway to peace is clear: first, we must acknowledge that seed of peace within us, and within one another. Then we must choose to quicken it with our intention, to nourish it with our heart-felt desire, and to carry it into practical action. Then truly the spirit of peace comes alive in us and around us.

Sometimes, though, having a clear pathway laid out before us is not enough. Sometimes we need help knowing how to follow the twists and turns of the trail, and what to do along the way to bring success to our journey. It is for that reason that The Peace Company is pleased to partner with Peace Cereal and several other organiza-tions to offer a nationwide initiative called Celebrate Peace!

You can read a description of this program on the following pages, and learn more about the partnering organizations later in this book. One of our contributions to this initiative is this *Celebrate Peace* book, a customized edition of our famed *The Peace Book: 108 Simple Ways to Make a More Peaceful World*, with the addition of new material from Peace Cereal and the Celebrate Peace partners.

Like that book, more than 75,000 copies of which are in circula-tion, this special edition is meant as the focus of our Great Peace Give-Away—a grassroots movement to spread the message and tools of peace by gifting the book to family, friends, colleagues, custom-ers, and others in our lives. I am a strong believer that peace is the ultimate gift we can give one another, and that peace grows when we give it away.

Therefore I invite you, dear reader, to join me and all of us at The Peace Company in celebrating peace—go to www.celebratepeace. com to learn more about the programs and to find out where they may be offered near you. Further, I invite you to use this book both as a guide for yourself and a gift for others, to awaken that living spirit of peace inside, and to witness its presence and its power through your daily actions.

Let us, together, be that vanguard that chooses the path of peace as a way of life, for ourselves and for all who come after us. Let us celebrate peace and light the way, in the midst of all that rages around us in these times. Now, more than ever, we are called.

Louise Diamond
July 2005

PEACE CEREAL invites you to

celebratepeace

Peace Cereal is committed to promoting the transformative power of peace. We initiated the Celebrate Peace program to spread a hopeful message and to cultivate the practice of peace in daily life through a national series of workshops and other educational programs, musical celebrations, and an internet-based community.

We believe in the power of peace, and we witness peace every day, all around us. Peace begins with a choice, develops through practice, and spreads by example.

We are proud to name Louise Diamond as our Person of Peace for 2005, and we're collaborating with Louise and The Peace Company to present their *Becoming a Peacebuilder* workshop and to make this wonderful book widely available.

We encourage you to share this book with others and to pass along the living spirit of Peace.

For more information about Celebrate Peace events and other peace-related resources visit **www.celebratepeace.com**
For more information about creating peace with Peace Cereal, visit **www.peacecereal.com**

in your heart

peace

in your home

in the world

PEACE
CEREAL.

donates at least 10% of our profits to organizations working on behalf of peace, representing over $1 million in donations over the past decade. By supporting peaceful activities we hope to inspire people to embrace peace.

The following are some of the organizations we have provided grants to over the past ten years. We encourage you to visit their websites to learn about their wonderful work and be inspired by their example.

Action Against Hunger	www.actionagainsthunger.org
Airline Ambassadors	www.airlineambassadors.org
American Friends Service Committee	www.afsc.org
East Meets West Foundation	www.eastmeetswest.org
Family Violence Prevention Fund	www.endabuse.org
Food From the Hood	www.foodfromthehood.com
Free The Children	www.freethechildren.org
Medicines Global	www.medicinesglobal.org
Peace Brigades International	www.peacebrigades.org
PEACE X PEACE	www.peacexpeace.org
PeaceJam	www.peacejam.org
Physician's Committee for Responsible Medicine	www.pcrm.org
Rainforest Alliance	www.rainforestalliance.org
The Ocean Conservancy	www.oceanconservancy.org

A Reader's Guide to
Celebrate Peace

Celebrate Peace, though small, is particularly dense with ideas and wisdom that can change your life. Reading it can be a great adventure, a discovery process, a doorway to a new you. Each of the 108 ways to build a culture of peace described here could have a whole book written about it—and some have! If you consider each one a gem, and take the time to absorb it fully, you just might find that something very special happens for you.

This book will come to, and affect, each reader in a different way. Perhaps you picked this book up at a retail shop or a friend gave it to you. Perhaps you found it on the seat of your pew one day at church, or it arrived in the mail with a nice note from your mother. However you received this book, know that it came to you for a reason.

To discover more about that reason, here are seven ways you might approach *Celebrate Peace:*

1 Hold it in your hands, and notice how it makes you feel.

2 Read the Table of Contents. Notice which items catch your attention. Before you turn to read more about those topics, stay with the simple words of the listing in the Table of Contents. See what comes to your mind, how you would fill out the details on that particular subject.

3 From the Table of Contents, pick one chapter or one topic that particularly jumps out at you. Turn immediately to that page, and read the message. Stop at the end, before you go on to another topic, and just sit with what you've read. What does it mean to you? How might it affect your life?

4 Browse and graze. Just open the book at random, and read whatever page you open to. Or, flip through the pages until something catches your eye. Trust that whatever you are drawn to is just the right message for you in that moment.

5 Start at the beginning and read straight through. You might do a chapter or two each day, or even finish the book in one sitting! Highlight or underline passages that you especially want to remember or come back to.

6 Read this book with your mind and with your heart. Use your eyes, and also your soul, to penetrate the meaning of the words. Notice which suggestions you just glide over, and which tug at you; which ones feel old and familiar, and which are startlingly new; which you have strong reactions to, and which seem so obvious that they hardly keep your attention.

7 Keep an ongoing list of which of the 108 tips for building a culture of peace you especially want to try. Review your list, and pick one to start with.

CONTENTS

INTRODUCTION
Changing Our Minds about Peace

Imagine all the people, living life in peace. . . .
—JOHN LENNON

IMAGINE

Imagine a world where:

- Children practice playground diplomacy, settling their own disputes peaceably, without fighting and without guns.

- The technology for peace is as big a business as the technology for war.

- Rival gang leaders sign a peace treaty and turn their attention to helping youth find jobs.

- Ideological opponents search for common ground on controversial issues, and work together to solve the problem.

- You can attend a university whose whole curriculum specializes in peace studies.

- Political and religious leaders apologize for oppression of racial or ethnic groups, and seek ways to right the wrongs.

· Movies, songs, games, television, books, newspapers, and magazines all portray peaceful resolution of conflicts as the "in" thing—full of drama, excitement, joy, and satisfaction.

· Governments have cabinet-level Departments of Peace.

Can you imagine such a world? Wouldn't it be wonderful if the values of peace were so deep in our culture that they were routinely expressed in these and countless other ways?

In fact, many of these are already happening, in small pockets around the world. The rest exist as seeds, planted in the minds of pioneers, waiting to find fertile soil in the ground of our society in order to grow and blossom.

Think of this book as the watering can.

WHAT IS PEACE?

This book is about peace. What does that mean? Peace is more than the absence of war, violence, or conflict, though that is an important first step. Peace is a presence—the presence of connection.

Inner peace is about connection with our true and natural self and a sense of being part of something larger. This connection gives rise to serenity, balance, and a feeling of well-being.

Peace with others is about our connection with the open heart, through which we remember our shared humanness. This brings us to the practice of conflict resolution, forgiveness, and reconciliation.

Peace in our communities and in the world requires a connection to respect for our multiple differences, and for the right of all people to justice, freedom, and dignity. This leads to trust, community, and co-existence.

Peace is a state of mind and a path of action. It is a concept, a goal, an experience, a path. Peace is an ideal. It is both intangible and concrete, complex and simple, exciting and calming. Peace is personal and political; it is spiritual and practical, local and global. It is a process and an outcome, and above all a way of being.

Ultimately, peace is about the quality of our relationships—with ourselves and with others. How can we live together, in the smallest individual and family units and in the largest networks of peoples and nations, in ways that honor who we are as dignified human beings? Think of this book as addressing that question, as an inquiry into the rich and varied nature and meaning of peace.

WHY PEACE? WHY NOW?

When the World Trade Center went down, something basic shifted in our human consciousness, at least in the United States: we woke up to the realities of war, and to the need for peace as a tangible presence among the whole human family. We woke up, too, to the realization that peace does not appear effortlessly, through our dreams—it requires action.

This seed has dropped onto fertile ground, prepared over the years by many events and trends. About thirty years ago we began to notice our relationship to the environment. We started to realize the need to preserve the natural world through individual and collective action. Now we are becoming aware of a similar need concerning our relationships with each other. More and more, we are taking responsibility to promote peace in our personal, national, and global lives together.

The United Nations declared the year 2000 as the UN Year of the Culture of Peace, and the years 2001 to 2010 the UN Decade for the Culture of Peace and Nonviolence for the Children of the World. As we enter a new millennium, we have the opportunity to examine where we have been as a human family, and where we are going. This is a precious and powerful moment. In these opening days and years of the twenty-first century, we can lay down a vision for our collective future and a program for how to get there.

Sadly, the events of the past century have shown us the immense destructive power we hold in our hands. The twentieth century was unsurpassed in human history in the sheer numbers of people killed, maimed, and rendered homeless by our acts of violence toward one another. And those are only the victims we can see and count. There are also millions of people around the world suffering from the everyday violence that comes with corruption, oppression, and injustice.

In the United States, children kill children; racism, sexism, and homophobia continue to flourish; rifts between ethnic and ideological groups widen; violence is the daily fare of our media and popular culture; historical wounds continue to fester; and the gap between rich and poor grows bigger.

The moment has come for everyday people in their everyday lives to wake up and say, "It's time to choose a better way; it's time to choose peace as the path to our children's future."

CHOOSING A BETTER WAY

Choosing a better way means changing our minds about peace. Because our actions naturally flow from our thoughts (our attitudes and assumptions), we have to change our minds if we want a different result .

But first we have to ask, "A better way than what?" Right now, we live in a society where many of the norms—assumptions about what is natural and acceptable—are anti-peace; that is, they promote distrust, disrespect, conflict, suffering, and the degradation of our human and natural resources.

These norms run so deep in our institutions and our daily lives that we may not even be aware of them. We just accept them "as the way things are." For instance, we accept that adversarial relationships ("us" against "them") are normal; that competition (I win, you lose) is universally good. We polarize our differences as right versus wrong, or good versus evil. We think we have the right to enforce our wishes on others, and live as if some of us are more entitled or privileged than others. We accept violence as a way of life and entertainment. Some of the worst ills that plague our society can be traced directly to these assumptions.

THE FOUR PRINCIPLES OF PEACE

A rapidly growing number of people are working to make a different set of assumptions our shared reality. A true culture of peace is based on four basic principles that promote trust, harmony, and healthy human relationships. These are

1 COMMUNITY   We come-in-unity first with ourselves, then with others, acknowledging we are all in this together, interconnected and interdependent. Therefore, what hurts one hurts all. Mutual respect, appreciation of differences, and honoring the equal dignity

and worth of all are expressions of this awareness, as is a commitment to social and economic justice.

2 COOPERATION   By finding common ground and working together, we can all "win." If we think of ourselves as partners and share our resources fully, we can find creative solutions to our joint problems and build bridges across whatever seems to divide us.

3 NONVIOLENCE   Respect for life and all individuals leads to a commitment not to harm others. We choose not to use force and coercion as a basis for relationship, but rather to relate to the goodness in each and every person. By keeping an open heart, we develop empathy and compassion. With dialogue and creative problem solving—and with a moral conviction to avoid the suffering caused by violence—we can address the toughest issues of our individual and collective lives.

4 WITNESS   Peace is a living presence within all of us. Like Justice, Freedom, Beauty, or Harmony, Peace is an ideal with a capital letter. It is encoded in us as natural wisdom, our spiritual birthright. Our job is to witness this truth by being the peace we seek, helping each other remember to live the ideal of peace in practical ways every day. We do this by relating to the potential for peace in every situation, and to the seed of peace in every person.

If these became the operating principles of our society, we might expect to see a vast reduction in crime and warfare. Our political discourse would be far more civil and more productive. Our historical wounds could mend, and our children could grow in safety. Our culture, in honoring peace, would be life affirming in every way.

WELCOME TO THE PEACE REVOLUTION

This book is an invitation to each and every person who picks it up: Come and join this revolutionary moment, and help make peace a way of life. By our individual and collective action, we can make the UN Decade of the Culture of Peace more than a high-sounding declaration; we can make it a turning point in human history, a doorway to a truly new millennium. We can make a peace revolution.

This book contains 108 very practical steps that anyone can take in their daily lives to express the Four Principles of Peace. The 108 ways are divided into twelve categories that describe various aspects of our lives. Of course there are far more than 108 things we can do for peace—the number is limited only by our imaginations. However, since every journey starts with a single step, if you practice even one of these 108 ways, you will have made a personal contribution to the peace revolution; you will have made a difference.

The book is meant to be given away to as large a number of people as possible so that the cumulative effects of our actions can produce an exponential change in our local, national, and global lives. Together, we have the power to make an historic shift that will benefit the family of life on this planet for generations to come.

See the final section of this book, on the Great Peace Give-Away, to see how you can be a part of this unique initiative.

Our children and our grandchildren will thank us.

Welcome, and enjoy!

CELEBRATE PEACE

108 Simple Ways to Create a More Peaceful World

INNER PEACE
Let Peace Begin With Me

Let there be peace on earth, and let it begin with me. . . .
A POPULAR SONG

The search for inner peace is the search for our natural self. The natural self lies beyond our particular personality. It is the core of our being, where we are innocent, loving, and fully present, like a newborn baby. This is the place where we touch the essence of life itself.

To find our natural self, we must learn to calm the inner battles and struggles we so often face. We must also learn to touch, at will, that deep pool of serenity and clarity that is the soul's birthright. To do either of these, we first need to slow down—way down.

We need to quiet the chatter and clutter in our minds so we can remember our true nature, like parting the clouds to find the deep blue sky, empty and endless. Here, in this place, we are wise, joyful, vibrantly alive—we are who we are meant to be, whole and holy, at peace, in peace, radiating peace, like the ripples of a pebble tossed into a lake. This is where all is possible, and everything begins.

1 BREATHE

Life is becoming faster and more stressful. Many of us live cut off from the natural world, dependent on machines and complex technologies. In our rush to keep up, we forget how important the simple act of breathing can be.

Breath is life. Breathing is nature's way of renewal. We release stale energy and feed ourselves with life force. Shallow or tight breathing makes us sick; full and easy breath keeps us healthy.

Usually we are not aware of our breathing. But when we turn our attention to it, something magical happens—our breath becomes slower, deeper, and we sink into a different state of consciousness.

- Sit comfortably, in a quiet place, and pay attention to your breathing. Say to yourself, "Now I'm breathing in; now I'm breathing out," as you follow that process in your body. Feel the circular flow, as the out-breath turns and becomes the in-breath, and vice versa. Feel the slowing down, the relaxation and letting go, the increase in well-being.

- Notice your mind wandering? That's normal. When you lose your focus on the breath, gently bring your attention back, and continue to watch the breath, moving in, moving out.

- Now add words. When breathing in, say, "I am filling with life, with all that is new and fresh." When breathing out, you might say, "I am releasing busy-ness of mind, all that is tight or stale."

- Sense or imagine this happening throughout your body—each cell, each atom, is being cleansed and refreshed by this flow of breath. You are literally "letting in a breath of fresh air."

2 RELAX

Stress builds up in our bodies. When we relax, we release the hurry, the worry, and the tightness that accumulate in our muscles and our minds. Relaxing is a way of letting go, of sinking easily into our natural self.

• Tighten and release all your muscle groups. Sitting or lying comfortably, start with your feet and ankles. Tighten all the muscles in that part of your body, as tight as you can. Hold that tension, hold it, then release it with a strong out-breath. Pause to let the release be complete. Go through the rest of your body, isolating one area at a time to tighten and release, ending with your face and scalp. Breathe easily and let yourself enjoy the lightness and sense of well-being that comes with deep relaxation.

• Soften the hard places. Over the years we tend to develop "favorite" places in our bodies where we hold our tension—perhaps our shoulders, or face, or stomach. Every once in a while, stop whatever you are doing, and turn your attention to those tight spots, softening the tension held there.

• Relax with music. Find music that suggests calm and peacefulness to you. Take time in your busy life to listen to that music: listen while you're doing chores, listen before you fall asleep, stop everything and just listen. Give yourself to the music, and let it carry you to a place of deep serenity.

• Relax with water. Water is soothing to body and soul. Take a hot bath or shower, a sauna, a Jacuzzi, a hot tub. Float in your favorite lake or pool. Dangle your feet in a stream. Walk along the beach and listen to the waves.

3   BE FULLY PRESENT

This moment is what there is; right here is where we are. There's no need to live in the past or the future; no need to be elsewhere. Being present to the present grounds and centers us. This is home, the source of inner peace. When we are home, in the here and now, everything is possible.

Centering ourselves in this home space requires the practice of mindfulness. Being mindful simply means paying attention. Whatever you are doing, pay full attention to it. By being mindful, you are awakening the natural self.

• Be centered physically. Sense the area just below your navel. This is your physical center, where you are connected to the life force. Lean forward and back, side to side, to feel when you get off center, and how you can come back again. This is home base.

• Be centered mentally. Whatever you are doing, focus on it 100 percent. As your mind begins naturally to wander into the past or the future, gently bring it back to this moment, to now, to whatever your activity may be. This is home base.

• Be centered emotionally. Whatever you are feeling, feel it fully, without judgment. Emotions have a natural rhythm—they arise, crest, and fall away, like a wave. Find the stillness from which all feelings arise, and to which you return as they pass. This is also home base.

• Be centered spiritually. Imagine that through your physical, mental, and emotional centers you are connected to the center of all other living beings—every human, plant, animal, even the earth and stars. This, too, is home base.

• Live from home base as much as you can. Whenever you go somewhere else, come back home as soon as possible.

4   LET NATURE NOURISH YOU

Nature is our direct line to inner peace. Though there can be great turmoil in the natural world (floods, earthquakes, the hunting and eating of prey), there are also endless settings of tranquility and beauty. When we steep ourselves in nature, we remember our connection to life itself, pure and simple. No matter where we live, we all have access to nature in some form.

• Go to unspoiled places as often as possible—the woods, the ocean, a river, a desert, a mountain, a meadow, a park.

• Wherever you are, use your senses to engage with the natural world. Touch a tree, smell a flower, catch a raindrop, hear the birds, or feel the sun against your face.

• You can also remember or create a place of natural beauty in your imagination.

· Whether physically or mentally, see, hear, and touch the majesty and mystery of nature. Experience the beauty, the wonder, and the awe of this miracle of life. Breathe deeply, relax into it.

· Let Mother Nature embrace you, and feed your soul. Know yourself to be a part of this natural world, not apart from it. Think of yourself as the tree, the flower, the butterfly.

· Notice how you feel. You can go to this place whenever you want—wherever you are, you can remember this experience, and recall that sense of being one with life.

5   COMMIT TO A PERSONAL PEACE PROCESS

We all have inner struggles. One part of us does battle with another. Finding inner peace means making peace with ourselves, a process that takes time and commitment.

We let ourselves be ruled by lists of shoulds and shouldn'ts, coulds and couldn'ts. We carry blame, shame, and guilt for what we've done or failed to do, how we've been or failed to be. We fill our minds with negative thoughts. We are afraid of many things, large and small. We even say and do mean things to ourselves.

We can learn our life's lessons without being at war with ourselves. We can choose to be in a personal peace process, resolving the conflicts that disturb our inner balance and harmony.

· Acknowledge a conflict you are having with yourself, and make a commitment to resolve it.

· Think of approaching your inner battle as a doctor giving medicine to the wounded. Each wound requires a different kind of medicine. Find the medicine that works for you: self-forgiveness for the wound of self-blame, compassion for shame, understanding for guilt, acceptance for judgment, trust for doubt.

· Face your fears. Think of something you fear in this moment. Now connect with your natural self (using the tools already described), and think of it again. Reach through the appearance to the essence—part the clouds to see the sky. What is there, really, to be afraid of?

• Practice fearlessness. Imagine the worst thing that could happen in your fear scenario. Instead of recoiling from it, try embracing it. Can you accept it? Could you survive it? If so, then you have discovered fearlessness. Think of an image or key word that will help you remember this experience whenever necessary.

6 PRACTICE THE ARTS OF INNER PEACE

The arts are a time-honored doorway to inner peace. We don't have to be "artists" in the traditional sense to experience the powerful connection we make when we participate in creative expression.

The arts take us beyond our small self, to a universal realm of beauty, harmony, and flow. They transport us to a larger dimension of who we are. Above all, they bring us to an appreciation of the ongoing process of creation and to our central role in it. Here, as with nature, we are deeply nourished.

• Playing an instrument, singing, or listening to a concert or recording, feel the power of sound. Be aware of the rhythms, the mood, the flow of notes; notice the interplay of harmonies, the dance of the different voices. Let all thoughts fade, and simply let the music be in you.

• Watching a dance performance, or dancing to your favorite music, feel the power of movement. Notice the natural stream of stretching and reaching, of flexing and contracting. Pay attention to how the energy moves through the body, with grace and ease, and to how the body interacts with the space around it.

• Whether looking at a favorite object in an art gallery or museum, or creating your own with crayons, colored pencils, markers, paints, clay, or other favorite medium, feel the power of image. Notice the colors, textures, lines, and shapes. Become the artist, the work of art, and the process of creating the art all at the same time.

• Reading or writing poetry, stories, or personal reflection, feel the power of words. Notice how the words come together in unique combinations, weaving a world of wisdom, meaning, and discovery. Find a passage that particularly inspires you, and read it often.

7   LISTEN TO THE INNER VOICE

When we connect with the natural self, beyond our fears and inner battles, we discover a different source of wisdom. Beneath the busyness, the stress, the everyday stories we tell ourselves lies a different way of knowing. When we penetrate the layers of our usual state of mind, using the methods presented so far, we find what has been called "the still small voice within."

This inner voice has many names—intuition, inner wisdom, the voice of God, spiritual guidance, higher power, beginner's mind, natural knowing. Whatever name we give it, the experience is the same. We begin to have access to new ideas, clear understandings, intuitive perceptions, hunches, visions of what is possible. Thoughts arise from somewhere deep within.

We all have different ways of experiencing this. Some see pictures or images; some hear actual words or messages. Some get glimpses of possibilities. Some see a plan of action unfolding. We may experience a great "Aha!" or simply have a sense of knowing.

This wisdom may not make sense from our normal frame of reference, or it might. Our task is to learn first to hear and then to trust this voice. It is our bridge from inner peace to outer action.

• Each morning, take five minutes to reconnect with your natural self, using any of the tools suggested here. Stay in that place, alert and aware, and simply notice what thoughts arise. Write down three or four that particularly catch your attention.

• Act on these thoughts during the day in some way, large or small.

• Check back in with yourself at bedtime. What did you notice? Was the wisdom that emerged useful?

8   LIVE ON PURPOSE

Our souls hunger for meaning. Why are we here? What is our life's purpose? In the bustle of modern society, we often forget to ask these questions until we are so tired, frustrated, or depressed that life seems to have lost its joy.

The meaning of life is not to be found outside, but from within. By listening to our inner voice, we begin to find our steps directed toward those activities and qualities of character that best express what we are here to be and do. We discover our potential for being all we can be, and the resources we already have for realizing this potential. We have a vision of where we want to go, and how to get there. We learn to live "on purpose."

· Make your own set of Life Purpose cards. Think of 12 (or more) values or qualities—like honesty, love, helping others—that are important to you. Write each one on a separate 3 × 5 card. Each day, pick one and dedicate your thoughts and actions for the day to living it fully.

· Get in the habit of asking questions of your natural self. "What greater good can I serve in this situation?" "What part of me needs to grow stronger?" "What is my path?" "What is the best course of action in this moment?" "What can I learn from this experience?"

· Listen for the response. It may not come immediately. It may not come in a straightforward, obvious form. But it will come, if you ask sincerely and listen patiently, trusting the inner voice.

· When you get some response to your question, act on it. Use your gift of free will to choose a course of action that honors the vision and purpose you are unfolding.

9 BROADCAST FROM THE PEACE FREQUENCY

Life is energy; peace is energy. Think of radio waves. There are different frequencies, or rates of vibration, on which you can broadcast your program. Anyone who tunes in to that frequency will receive whatever you are sending. If you are vibrating with anger, frustration, or pain, that is what others around you will receive. If you are vibrating with peace, then you are sending that message to all you meet.

Peace has its own frequency, or quality of consciousness. If you practice enough, you will come to recognize how it feels inside—the energy or vibratory signature of inner peace. Then, as with a radio, you can turn up the volume. You can choose to radiate this energy near and far, to broadcast from your own peace radio station. Finding inner peace, then, becomes an act of great generosity and love, when you share it with others simply by being who you are.

· Practice dropping in to a state of inner peace at will, using the techniques described here, or whatever else works for you.

· Next time you find yourself in a tense situation, go home to this place of peace and radiate that sense of well-being and serenity. You don't need to say or do anything outwardly—just simply be peace, and let it shine from within you.

· Hold this without distraction for as long as you can. What happens? How does the situation change? How do others respond?

· Think of a situation further away, to which you would like to contribute the energy of peace. From your place of inner peace, reach out to embrace the situation you are thinking about. Send out waves of peace from your heart.

REVIEW

Practice the Four Principles of Inner Peace

COMMUNITY
Feel the connection with your natural self.

COOPERATION
Trust your inner voice, and work with it.

NONVIOLENCE
Reduce the stress in your life, and address your inner conflicts lovingly.

WITNESS
Be radiant with the presence of peace.

FIRST LIGHT

The beauty and majesty of the natural world easily inspire inner peace. This is especially true when we are able to be quietly present with the elements. The man in this story gave himself over to the experience of the mountains, and was richly rewarded.

Hot, dry, dusty late summer, and the abandoned mines lend a feeling of the Old West here in New York State. Four of us set off for another adventure in the mountains. Memories of earlier trips linger—the time the lightning struck all around us, as the heavens opened up on our secret camp tucked into the hills; getting lost in the maze of beaver canals; the baby rattlesnake we found in our path.

The trail gently carries us skyward. A long, brown, furry animal bounds in front of us, stopping to sniff an old deer trail. A red squirrel complains to the neighborhood. In that storm of sound, I find the crest of a wave of calm.

We leave the trail, climbing a steep slope to traverse the ridge and find a place to camp. Spruce thickets become more dense; we find signs of bear. We reach camp at sunset, torn up from the brambles, tired and hungry. We bake bread over the hot coals under a starry sky.

Morning brings a most beautiful discovery. I wander up the river, pretending I'm a mink, bouncing and springing up the rocky shore. The wide open banks are so inviting after being lost in the spruce forest yesterday. I notice the sunlight is just about to strike somewhere on the river shore. Where will first light hit? I guess, and position myself there to watch. Looking softly, and as wide as I can, I find the western peaks glowing in the sunrise. I am sitting in a cozy cutaway in the rock, with a cedar growing right above me, and the first light of the day strikes just here. Drinking in the river sounds, I know that nature is infinite—and so am I.

RESOURCE GUIDE

PROGRAMS AND ORGANIZATIONS

Check in your local community for programs on stress reduction, relaxation, meditation, and similar activities. Yoga, dance, or martial arts classes might also help in finding inner peace. Here are some suggestions:

INSIGHT MEDITATION SOCIETY

A retreat center for silent meditation practice, on 80 wooded acres in the quiet country of central Massachusetts. Insight Meditation (Vipassana) is a simple and direct practice—the moment-to-moment observation of the mind/body process through calm and focused awareness. Growth in clarity increases peace in our daily lives.

BARRE, MA; PHONE: 978-355-4378; FAX: 978-355-63-98;
WEB SITE: www.dharma.org

KIRKRIDGE RETREAT CENTER

A retreat center located on a mountain ridge with great vistas, providing rest and renewal, a haven from the whirling world. Offers 55 retreats annually, including retreats on peacemaking, diversity, and other topics.

BANGOR, PA; PHONE: 610-588-1793; WEB SITE: www.kirkridge.org

STRESS REDUCTION CLINIC

Offers an outpatient mind/body-oriented, mindfulness-based stress reduction program in the form of an eight-week course that you can take as a complement to whatever medical treatments you may be receiving. This is the oldest and largest hospital-based stress reduction clinic in the world, with a solid base of clinical studies and research findings to support its work.

WORCESTER, MA; PHONE: 508-856-8999;
E-MAIL: mindfulness@umassmed.edu;
WEB SITE: www.umassmed.edu/cfm

BOOKS, TAPES, VIDEOS

The Act of Mindful Living: How to Bring Love, Compassion and Inner Peace into Your Daily Life. Thich Nhat Hanh, audiocassette, TNH, 1992.

Aquarian Times, the Kundalini Yoga Magazine. Aquarian Times offers transformative yogic technology and wisdom for accelerating personal excellence. Including practical tips and tools for health and happiness, *Aquarian Times* strives to be a voice of change, a promoter of peace, and a powerful tool for healing and uplifting humanity.

Attaining Inner Peace: Practical Applications of A Course in Miracles. Gerald G. Jampolsky, M.D., Diane V. Cirincione, audiocassette, 1993.

Finding Peace: Letting Go and Liking It. Paula Peisner Coxe, Sourcebooks, Inc., 1994.

Inner Peace Music. Steven Halpern, www.innerpeacemusic.com

A Path to Peace: Finding Inner Peace in Daily Life. Christopher Jackson, audiocassette, 1999.

Snatam Kaur. Her *Celebrate Peace* CD is a musical celebration of the spirit of peace. Available at www.spiritvoyage.com/peace.

The Stress Reduction Workbook. Available online at www.stress-institute.com.

WEB SITES
Inner Self MAGAZINE

Dedicated to discovering wisdom, peace, and joy in our daily lives. www.innerself.com

MINDFULNESS-BASED STRESS REDUCTION

Workshops, discussions, resources, books, and products for Mindfulness-Based Stress Reduction. www.mbsr.com

Keywords to explore using your computer search engine: *stress reduction, mind/body stress reduction, stress management, inner peace.*

PEACE WITH FAMILY & FRIENDS
Conflict Resolution Made Easy

Make new friends, but keep the old,
One is silver and the other gold.
A POPULAR SONG

Our best opportunity to practice the Four Principles of Peace is with family and friends. We are more vulnerable in our relationships with those who are closest to us, more likely to hurt and be hurt while we seek to love and be loved.

Here is where we can perfect the art of conflict resolution. Indeed, if we do not find ways to prevent, clear, and heal the inevitable hard feelings that arise from time to time, these relationships will sour. We must be watchful, tending our loved ones like a garden, lest the weeds spread and choke off the growth. We must pull the weeds before they become too dense, for once they've taken over, the work is much harder and the plants weakened.

10 REMEMBER THE REASON
FOR THE RELATIONSHIP

People are in our lives for a reason. Parents, siblings, and children, intimate partners and best friends—they all provide a laboratory for growing in love. They touch the deepest places in us and we in them. These are the relationships that shape our personalities, our life paths, our souls' unfolding. They are precious.

They also anchor us in the human family. They provide us with the experience of relatedness, community, and intimacy. Without them we would be alone. With them, we learn what it means to be a son or daughter, mother or father, sister or brother, lover, and friend.

When things are difficult between us, therefore, it is important to remember the purpose of our being together and to hold that as our reference point. This puts the inevitable frustrations, hurts, and disappointments into a larger context. It gives us a light to aim for, like a candle in the window, reminding us where home is on a dark night.

· Think about those people closest to you, one by one. Why are they in your life? What do you learn from them about yourself? About life? About love? Why are they important to you?

· Pick one person—family member or friend—with whom you are very close. Recall when a cloud came between you, some harsh word or act, some failure to care. Now remember why this person is important to you, what the ideal of your relationship is. What do you notice?

· Now try it out in real life. The next time you have difficulty with a loved one, look at them and remember who they really are to you. Relate to them from that point of view. Put the conflict in that context, and see what happens.

11 SEE CONFLICT AS OPPORTUNITY

Conflict is a natural part of life. It is inevitable. We have disagreements with the people we love because of our differences—our different natures, life experiences, and outlooks—and because of our vulnerability. Those disagreements, however, do not need to escalate into serious fights. We can prevent that by using conflict as an opportunity to learn and grow.

Our friends and families are the ones who help us meet our basic human needs for safety and survival, self-esteem, belonging, and growth. They are our intimate partners, those who know our strengths and weaknesses, our tender places and hot spots. Therefore the conflicts we are likely to have with them are more personal than those with strangers, and more threatening.

The greater the threat, the greater the lesson. These conflicts are like the sand in the oyster around which the pearl grows; they are the seed for learning our most important lessons about love and life, about ourselves and the other, about human relationship and community.

- Think of a current or recent conflict situation with someone you love. Ask yourself what the lesson in this situation is for you. What quality of character are you strengthening? What are you learning to let go of? What new skills or attitudes are you developing? How can you use this to grow?

- Embrace the lesson; accept it as a gift.

- Consider the person you are in conflict with as your teacher. Let yourself feel gratitude toward her, for giving you the opportunity to learn this lesson. Tell him, in your mind, how much you appreciate this gift. Tell her in person.

12   RELATE TO THE BASIC GOODNESS

We all carry a spark of the divine within us—a seed of basic goodness (or godliness). Our work is to grow this spark into a mighty flame. We can help ourselves and each other do this by choosing to acknowledge this basic goodness, even in the midst of conflict.

When we are hurt or angry with someone, we tend to think how bad or how wrong they are. We are sure they mean to hurt us, when really they are probably doing the best they can to take care of themselves. In our reaction, we tend to confuse their "being" with their "doing"; that is, we relate to what they do as if it were who they are.

We need to separate the two if we want to bring peace to the relationship. The behavior is not the person. The person is essentially fine; the behavior can be changed. By relating to the basic goodness in both ourselves and our conflict partners, we make it safe to examine and perhaps change the behavior while feeling valued and appreciated.

- Start by relating to the basic goodness in yourself. Find that spark within you. (Hint: If you're having trouble, look in your heart.) Acknowledge yourself as simply divine!

- Now do the same regarding someone you love. Find that spark in her. Appreciate it.

- Think of a difficulty you have had or are having with a loved one. Listen to the negative ways you describe him to yourself. Make the distinction between who he really is and what his behavior is—then listen to your inner dialogue again. Notice any difference? Does this change how you feel about the situation? What you can do about it?

13 LISTEN, WITH EMPATHY

Communication is the basic tool of relationship. Good listening is the cornerstone of good communication, because we all want and need to be heard. Listening is our way of hearing how the other person makes sense to herself. Understanding someone doesn't mean we necessarily agree with him. Not understanding leaves us open to argument and judgment.

Listening happens with more than the ears; it happens with the heart. We not only need to understand our friend, we also need to feel empathy with whatever she is feeling.

- Put aside, for now, your own opinions, reactions, stories, arguments, and urgency to talk, so you can be fully present to listen to your friend. You can go back to your own thoughts later.

- Give the speaker your full attention. Don't be rehearsing what you will say next, arguing in your mind with his opinions, or thinking about other things—focus completely on the one who is sharing. Receive his words as a gift, given in trust.

- Listen for the meaning (the story, the substance) and also listen for the feelings (the emotions, the concerns). Hear what she is really saying, not your own interpretation.

• Let your friend know you have heard her by giving back to her the main points of what she said and by acknowledging her feelings.

• Open your heart to understand how the situation looks and feels from his point of view.

• Ask questions that help the speaker go deeper. For instance, "What do you mean by that?" "How does that make you feel?" "What would you like to happen next?" Unlike "Yes" or "No" questions, these keep the conversation going, and show your interest.

14 SHARE, WITH STRAIGHT TALK

To be heard, you must share. This part of the communication is where you get to let the other person know how you make sense to yourself. The clearer you can be about the truth of your own experience, the easier it is for your friend to listen well and to understand.

The way to be clear is to stick to your own story. If you use your sharing as a way to hurt or blame the other, make yourself right and them wrong, or win points in an argument, they will likely become defensive and less able to really hear you.

• Tell the truth of your own experience. Simply. Directly. Tell it as you would tell a story. It is your story. You don't have to apologize for it or overdramatize it. Just speak it out straight; share it as a gift.

• Speak for yourself. Talk about what you think and feel, not what the other person did or didn't, should or shouldn't do, think or feel. Say, "I . . . ," not "You. . . ."

• Acknowledge your own point of view. What may seem like obvious facts to you are probably seen differently by someone else.

• Share both your thoughts and your feelings. Your thoughts are your beliefs, assumptions, and opinions—the rational meaning you give your experience. Your feelings are your emotions, your sensations, your hopes and concerns—the psychological meaning you give your experience. Both are important.

• Bring to the surface your assumptions, hidden beliefs, and fantasies. You draw certain conclusions because of what you assume or imagine to be true. Your friend can understand you better if she sees how you arrived at your conclusions—what data you considered, what conclusions you drew from that data. You can understand yourself better too.

15   STOP THE GAMES

When we repeat a pattern of relating to others again and again, it becomes a game. A game destroys peace between loved ones because it takes on a life of its own. If we are busy playing our familiar roles, we cannot be genuine with each other.

One common game is the victim/persecutor pattern. There are many others: the parent/child pattern; the bully/wimp pattern; the come close/go away pattern; the smart/stupid pattern. We are infinitely creative in finding ways to lock ourselves into familiar roles that limit our behavior.

• Notice your game patterns. When you're in a situation that feels familiar, ask yourself what this reminds you of, and look to see how you may be repeating a pattern and playing a role.

• Risk doing it differently. Break the pattern by experimenting with new behavior. If you are usually apologetic, be assertive; if you are often the one who knows everything, try being curious. If you're feeling sorry for yourself all the time, practice appreciation.

• Tell the story in a different way. We make sense of our experience by telling ourselves a story about it. We can get a new view by changing the story. If you've had a difficult situation with a loved one, tell yourself the story about what happened. Then tell about the same situation in a different way, from a new perspective. Notice how this changes your experience.

• Laugh together at your games. Identify your patterns with each other, and give them funny names. Then you can remind and help each other change the game by referring to those names. "Oh, there I go being a grump again." Or, "This is beginning to sound like our Snow White and Prince Charming routine."

16   KEEP LOVE FLOWING
THROUGH THE HARD TIMES

To sustain peace in our relationships, we need to keep our hearts open. The physical heart keeps blood pumping; the human heart keeps love flowing. If we harden our hearts against one another, love cannot flow. Our job is to keep the channels open so caring, appreciation, and trust can keep circulating between us.

• Clear the air. When something comes between you and your loved one—hurtful words or actions, disrespect, a lack of appreciation—deal with it as soon as possible. Don't let it fester.

• Take responsibility. We are 50 percent of every relationship, but we are 100 percent responsible for our half. When our actions stop the flow of love between us, we need to own up to our behavior and its harmful effects. It doesn't matter who started it; it only matters that we acknowledge our part in it.

• Apologize. Say "Sorry" when you have hurt your loved one. Ask for forgiveness. This is a sign of strength, not weakness. It shows you really care. It shows you recognize your responsibility. It allows your friend to let go, and it clears the air.

• Make amends. Sometimes saying "Sorry" is not enough to restore harmony. We may need to take action as well. A good basic premise: If something is broken, fix it.

• Forgive. If your friend says "Sorry"—or even if they don't—let go and forgive. Forgiving bad behavior doesn't mean condoning it; it only means you're ready to let go of your reaction to it, and reopen your heart.

• Hold trust as sacred. A fragile web of trust holds us together. Through intimacy, we are deeply vulnerable, and we rely on each other to keep us safe. Trust can take years to build, and only a single moment to destroy. Keeping confidences, honoring agreements, and cherishing the love and friendship as a precious gift will assure lasting trust.

17 COMMIT TO A WIN-WIN SOLUTION

In disputes with our loved ones, we have a basic choice. We can try to win the argument and come out on top, or we can work together for a mutually satisfactory solution. A win-lose approach may make one party feel good for the moment, but the loser will be left feeling sad, angry, or dissatisfied, which will harm the relationship. A win-win approach leaves everyone feeling good about the outcome and about the process for getting there.

· Think of the dispute as a joint problem to be solved together. You can get a better result if you are side by side, facing the problem, than if you are facing off against each other.

· Gather information. Take the time to listen and share, to gather all the information you need about the situation from both points of view.

· Look below the surface. Often, what we think we are fighting about is not really it at all. Beneath our stated positions, we have needs and concerns that we're trying to satisfy. Positions are hard to accommodate, because they may seem mutually exclusive; needs and concerns are easier to address because they are often shared or overlapping. It is in our own interest to satisfy each other's needs.

· Get creative. Work together to find several possible ways of meeting each other's needs. There is rarely only one way. Suggest many options, even if they may not seem realistic. In the process, you will likely find some that make sense and are doable.

· Make and keep agreements. Once you've found an option you like, follow through with action. Do what you said you would. Check in with each other to make sure the solutions are working. If so, congratulate yourselves! If not, try something else.

18   DEVELOP FAMILY RITUALS AND NORMS

We can reduce tensions and increase peace among loved ones by establishing positive habits and regular rituals. That way, everyone knows what to expect, and clear pathways for peace are established.

Norms are the behaviors and values we agree to that eventually become "how things are" in our relationships. Rituals are ceremonies that express our values and strengthen our positive norms through repetition and a sense of specialness.

• Show appreciation often. We all want to feel seen and heard, and know we're valued by our loved ones. You can make an everyday norm of showing your love and gratitude in simple ways—like saying, "Thank you," giving an unexpected little gift, letting your friend know that you especially appreciate or admire something they did or said. Conflicts are less likely to develop when we feel nourished by appreciation.

• Hold family councils. Having special times when members of the family get together to discuss what's on their minds can provide a way to both prevent and resolve conflicts. It creates a pattern of joint problem solving and provides a safe and encouraging space for everyone to listen (with empathy) and share (with straight talk).

• Create special peacemaking rituals. Apology, forgiveness, and making amends works easier when they are part of "how things are" in our families. Peacemaking rituals or ceremonies can be simple or elaborate—anything from a handshake or hug to a celebration with candles, food, and gifts. What's important is that we establish familiar, accepted, and repeated ways to regain our loving connection when we have lost it.

REVIEW

Practice the Four Principles of Peace in the Family

COMMUNITY
Communicate with love, to serve
the larger purpose of the relationship.

COOPERATION
Develop family rituals and norms
for peaceful resolution of conflicts.

NONVIOLENCE
Practice empathy.

WITNESS
Remember the basic goodness in everyone.

THE FAMILY DINNER

A simple ritual can bind even a hurting family together. The woman telling this story found a way, despite the pain of divorce, to keep her family connected in love through a simple weekly meal.

My husband and I divorced two years ago, and though we knew we couldn't be happy living together, we still shared a commitment to raising our two children together. We agreed to live geographically close to one another as long as the kids are in school, and we set up a somewhat flexible shared custody arrangement. We share expenses equally for the children.

We decided to have a weekly "family dinner" with just the four of us, so the kids could have the undivided attention of both parents for at least an hour a week. This was probably the most difficult agreement to keep when anger and hurt were the prevailing emotions, but it's also been the most rewarding. We are forced to set aside our adult issues for that hour and really concentrate on the children.

Most of the time dinners are what you would expect with a lively ten- and seven-year-old. "Ewww, I hate meatloaf!" "No more applesauce until you finish your broccoli." Discussions about the day: "What did you do in school today?" "Nothin'." Plans for the week, upcoming events, negotiations for the latest must-have acquisition. The routines of grade school life repeated like a catechism of normalcy. I really treasure those moments when my kids get to participate in a "regular" family meal. It's become a cherished ritual.

Family Dinner has also become the time when we can acknowledge our commitment to our children and celebrate their amazing, funny, and precious presence in our lives. I'm so proud of how my kids are managing the emotional roller coaster of a newly divided household, and I want to honor their ability to be healthy, normal, happy kids.

RESOURCE GUIDE

PROGRAMS AND ORGANIZATIONS

Check in your local community for programs on family life, communication skills, conflict resolution, and family mediation. Here are some suggestions:

CENTER FOR NONVIOLENT COMMUNICATION

A global organization helping people compassionately connect with themselves and one another through Nonviolent Communication, a process created by Marshall Rosenberg, Ph.D. Training is available through workshops, audio, video, written materials, games, and through the creation of schools based on the process of Nonviolent Communication.

SHERMAN, TX; PHONE: 903-893-3886: FAX: 903-893-2935: E-MAIL: cnvc@compuserve.com; WEB SITE:WWW.cnvc.org

PARENTING FOR PEACE AND JUSTICE NETWORK

Part of the Institute for Peace and Justice. An interfaith, interracial, transnational association of families who seek well-being, wholeness, peace, and justice in our living situations and in the broader community.

ST. LOUIS, MO; PHONE: 314-533-4445, FAX: 314-715-6455; E-MAIL: ipj@ipj-ppj.org; WEB SITE: www.ipj-ppj.org

BOOKS, TAPES, VIDEOS

Difficult Conversations: How to Discuss What Matters Most. Douglas Stone, Bruce Patton, Sheila Heen, and Roger Foster. Penguin USA, 2000.

The Eight Essential Steps to Conflict Resolution: Preserving Relationships at Work, at Home, and in the Community. Dudley Weeks. Putnam, 1994.

How To Talk So Kids Will Listen & Listen So Kids Will Talk. Adele Faber and Elaine Mazlish. Avon Books, 1980.

New Games for the Whole Family. Dale N. Lefevre. Perigee, 1988.

Nonviolent Communication. Marshall B. Rosenberg. Maylin H. Fisher, illustrator. Puddle Dancer Press, 1999.

WEB SITES

FAMILIES AGAINST VIOLENCE ADVOCACY NETWORK

Network of organizations, families, and individuals committed to violence prevention and the promotion of alternatives to violence in our families, schools, parishes, congregations, youth groups, colleges, and prisons.

www.ipj-ppj.org/favan.html

MAKE THE PEACE CAMPAIGN

Resources, curriculum, personal commitment forms, media tools, and more, for taking personal responsibility to make the peace. Suggestions for solving family, school, and community problems in a peaceful way.

www.makethepeace.org

WWW.MEDIATE.COM

Articles, resources and training focused on peace within family, marriage, between parents and children, including divorce.

www.mediate.com/fam

WWW.MEDIATORS.ORG

Offers books, brochures, videos, audiotapes, and other resources on mediation and conflict resolution for families.

www.mediators.org

Keywords to explore through your compute search engine: *nonviolent communication, conflict resolution, negotiation, family mediation.*

PEACE FOR THE CHILDREN
Priority Alert!

Our children
Are not our children;
They are the sons and the daughters of life
Longing for itself
—KAHLIL GIBRAN

T he greatest gift we can give to our children is to raise them in
a culture of peace. We don't have to be biological parents to
give this gift. We all have children in our lives, directly or indirectly. Through our extended families, our neighborhood schools and
playgrounds, the youth groups at our places of worship, or through our
local and national policies on children and education, we all have some
way to reach out and touch the lives of the next generation.

Raising a generation of children committed to peace as a way of
life should be our most urgent priority. What we learn as children, we
live as adults. When children learn violence—whether through video

games, emotional abuse, or ethnic warfare—they repeat that violent behavior as adults. If they learn early how to resolve their conflicts nonviolently, and how to respect the differences among us, they will carry these lessons into their future.

One of the strongest messages of peace we can send our children is to honor their true natures. If we ignore them, put them down, or fail to give them the time, attention, respect, and fascination they deserve, we are doing great violence to our children's souls. The children are our national treasure. They deserve the best of what we have to give.

19   COMMIT TO RAISING PEACEKEEPERS

Because we live in a culture of violence, children will not learn peace as a way of life without special effort on our part. We must make it our conscious goal to raise our children as peacekeepers—as human beings who can live the Four Principles of Peace as naturally as they breathe.

Choosing to raise our children as peacekeepers is a big responsibility. It requires the courage to be "different" and to have our children seen as "different" in a dominant culture that's so competitive and adversarial. It means being creative, because we don't yet have, as a society, a tool box full of ways to live the Four Principles of Peace. It requires commitment, day by day, to set the values, skills, and behaviors of the peacekeeper at the top of the list of what's important for us and for our children.

- Tell the children in your life that you are committed to raising them as peacekeepers. Share with them why this is important to you. Make the Four Principles of Peace part of the daily conversation. Put up a poster of the Principles on a wall in your home.

- Let other significant adults in the lives of your children know that the path of the peacekeeper is important to you—teachers, family members, parents of the children's friends. Educate them about what this means to you. Give away posters of the Four Principles of Peace. (You can get posters of the Four Principles of Peace from PeaceTech, at 1-888-455-5355 or *www.peace-tech.com*.)

• Let your children know clearly what is expected of them as peacekeepers. Let them know you are pleased every time they demonstrate peacekeeping behavior.

• Practice daily "show and tell" with the Four Principles of Peace—show by your own behavior, and tell by guiding the actions of your children into those channels.

20   SET THE EXAMPLE

Children learn from what they see. Young children, especially, imitate their parents' values and behaviors. If they see us using force to get what we want, they will do the same. If they see us managing our feelings and our differences comfortably, they will take it for granted that problems can be solved in a friendly way.

We often think that telling our children how to behave is what will teach them right from wrong, but we forget that our own behavior is their most important schoolroom. If we tell our son not to hit his friends when he is angry, and then spank him when we are angry with him, he will learn to believe his experience rather than our words. If we tell our daughter not to make fun of people who are different from her, and then call our neighbors a nasty name when they upset us, she will think it's okay to use language to hurt.

• Pay attention to where violence—any form at all of hurting or belittling others—is part of your daily life. Make a conscious choice to change this behavior as a gift to your children.

• Notice especially how you use your voice: yelling, cursing, put-downs (of yourself or others), nasty remarks, negative judgments, an angry tone of voice, interrupting another's communication, even jesting ("I could just kill you!") are also forms of violence.

• Let your children know that you yourself are learning to be more peaceful and working to create a culture of peace in your own life. Help them understand, through watching you, that learned behavior can be changed. Ask for their help in your own learning process.

• Practice with your children the forms of respect in word and deed that you expect from them.

21 STOP THE DAILY DIET OF VIOLENCE

To create a culture of peace for our children, we need to stop their daily exposure to violence. Every day, our children witness or experience violence in many forms: physically, where bodies are hurt; verbally, where self-esteem is hurt; emotionally, where hearts are hurt.

This violence is all around them: on television, in movies, in music, in toy stores, on the playground, in classrooms, in homes. It has become normative—part of the accepted fabric of life, as "the way things are."

- Break the silence. We do not control all of the vehicles of violence, so we cannot stop it altogether. We can, however, withdraw our consent to it. Our silence supports the culture of violence. Breaking the silence to say, "That's not how we do things in this family (classroom, youth group)" helps create new norms.

- Turn off the television. At the very least, monitor closely what your children watch. Even cartoons show violence as normal. Do not take your children to movies that glamorize violence. Do not buy toy weapons. Talk with your children about why you are setting these limits.

- Educate children to be aware of the kinds of personal violence that can be done unthinkingly: put-downs, rudeness, disrespect for those who are different from us, shaming, blaming, and holding grudges, for example. Hold this behavior to be as unacceptable as hitting or kicking.

- Be courageous. You will be tested, over and over again, on this approach. Pressure from peers, from advertising media, from the general culture, will push you to reconsider your decision to limit your child's participation in the culture of violence. This will give you the opportunity to know your own boundaries, stand up for your beliefs, and be a role model of resolve for your children.

22 SUPPORT PEACE AT SCHOOL

Our children spend much of their waking hours in school. Through subject matter taught in the classroom, from peer interaction, and by how people treat each other—in class, in the cafeteria, in the halls, and on the playground—our children are being socialized every day, told which behaviors are acceptable and which are not. A consistent message at home and school about the culture of peace can give our children the support they need to follow the Four Principles of Peace.

• Support playground diplomacy. Many schools have peer mediation programs, where the children themselves help each other resolve disputes. If your school has such a program, find a way to get your child involved. Then learn the same techniques, so home and school are using the same methods of conflict resolution. If your school doesn't have such a program, lobby hard for one.

• Encourage schools to use the Four Principles of Peace as a daily teaching tool. Ask that it be displayed in every classroom; discussed regularly; used as a reference for appropriate and inappropriate behavior.

• Suggest assembly programs, teaching units, and field trips that highlight the message of nonviolence, human rights, conflict resolution, diversity, reconciliation, and tolerance.

• Request an educational approach that helps children learn they are global citizens. Let them study other cultures, world affairs, and current events. Encourage travel to other places, exchange student programs, and visits to refugee centers.

• Support approaches to history that focus less on wars and more on the peace processes that ended the wars; less on conquerors and more on the fate of the conquered; less on military heroes and more on the great peacemakers of the world.

• Strongly encourage cooperative, group-oriented approaches to both learning and playing. Team-based projects in school, and non-adversarial "new games" for play strengthen the values of cooperation and joint problem solving.

23   CREATE PEACE CORNERS

A peace corner is some chosen spot—in a classroom or a home— where anyone can go to experience a sense of peace and well-being. Here, a child can regain a sense of inner peace after an upset, bring a dispute to be settled, or take a moment to relax and reconnect with his or her natural self.

Children understand what adults value by what they see. By having a physical space that honors peace, we are saying, "This is important." The space is meant to be comfortable and to have a few simple objects that hand and eye can focus on to help bring us back to center.

· Ask the children to help you set up a peace corner in your home or classroom. Invite them to bring objects that give them a sense of peacefulness and connection. Soft pillows; beautiful nature pictures; gifts from the natural world, such as rocks, leaves, or feathers; magnetic poetry—there are many possible items that might go in your peace corner.

· Encourage the children to help keep the peace corner clean and fresh, with new objects added from time to time. Help them feel that this is their place, that they can care for it lovingly so it serves them.

· Work with the children to set the guidelines for the peace corner: how many people can be there at once, for how long; how you know when to go to the peace corner; and when you are ready to leave. Make sure the peace corner is never used for a time out or for any kind of punishment—it is a place of welcome and invitation. If disputes, concerns, or frustrations are resolved in the peace corner, have a consistent process or ritual that everyone knows.

· Include a journal book with writing and drawing materials, so children can reflect on whatever has brought them to the peace corner, and all who enter can enjoy the reflections.

· Use the peace corner yourself, so the children will see how you value it.

24 ENCOURAGE SAFE EXPRESSION OF FEELINGS

Learning to manage emotions safely and effectively is one of childhood's most critical lessons. A child's feelings are naturally close to the surface. Being mad, glad, sad, and afraid (with variations and combinations) are central to the child's experience as a human being.

Frustrations that build, needs that remain unsatisfied, concerns that are not addressed can lead to fighting, hurting, and various forms of acting out. We need to help our children know that feelings are okay, that we take them seriously, and that we can express them in ways that honor the Four Principles of Peace.

• Help children know what they're feeling. Give names to emotional states, so children can recognize what's going on for them on the inside, and use words to communicate.

• Acknowledge the validity of a child's feelings. "Of course you feel that way." Listen to what's behind the feelings. Make sure the child feels really heard, so they don't have to use inappropriate behavior to get the attention they need.

• Help children realize that they have choices in how to manage their feelings. Invite options from the child ("What could you do with that feeling?") or suggest some. Offer no shame for any feeling: boys can cry and girls can feel aggressive, even grown-ups feel scared or hurt sometimes.

• Get creative in helping children channel aggression and big hurts or frustrations in appropriate and even fun ways. Anger can turn into a growl, making faces, butting into a soft cushion; sadness can flow with tears, with drawing, with telling a story about what is sad and finding a happy ending.

• Find ways to avoid or distract from the build up of negative feelings. If you know your child gets cranky in the grocery store, give her a snack before you go shopping; if you see jealousy starting to come on because another child has something yours doesn't, turn his attention to something else.

• Let kids know they can have help dealing with really big feelings, especially in public places. If something starts to erupt, stop what you're doing and give the child your full and loving attention. Put aside your own sense of embarrassment if others are around, and help your child find words or acceptable actions for dealing with what they're feeling.

• Set expectations and limits for acceptable ways of expressing feelings, and stand behind them. Tailor it with and for each child. Let children know if they're out of bounds: "This is not the way we do this in our family (classroom, youth group)."

25 LISTEN, REALLY LISTEN

Children need the grown-ups in their lives to listen to them. They need to be seen and heard; they need to be acknowledged as beings in their own right, with their own likes and dislikes and ways of being in the world.

The simplest and single most effective tool we can use to support our children as peacekeepers is to listen to them. Whatever they are feeling, saying, or doing makes sense to them through their internal logic—which will almost certainly be different from ours. By taking the time to listen deeply to what's important to them, we help ground our kids in their natural selves, the source of both inner and outer peace.

• Give kids your undivided attention. Children live in their own worlds—they have their own friends, their own stories. They naturally want to share this with their parents, teachers, and grown-up friends. Take the time to be present to this sharing—with full and loving focus on the child.

• Listen actively, to understand what's really being communicated. What are the words saying? What are the feelings being expressed? What is important to the child in this communication? What is he trying to get across to you?

• Let the child know you have really heard what she was trying to share. Often, a child doesn't need you to do anything with what they say, only to really hear it. Reflect back to her what you did hear, and check to see if you got the message right.

• Make the distinction between listening and agreeing; between sharing and demanding. If it is important to your child to have the new toy he sees in the store, you can listen to the request and honor it as a desire, without having to fulfill it.

26 GIVE TEENAGERS A SAFE SPACE

Adolescence is a different and difficult world. Teens and preteens are going through so many changes that they may need a particular kind of safety to stay on the peace path. They also have greater access to resources, influences, and opportunities for stepping away from the Four Principles of Peace.

Teenagers are especially working with the tension of identity. They are learning how to be uniquely themselves and still be part of the crowd. They are questioning the values, goals, and beliefs they grew up with, to sort out what they will carry into adulthood and what leave behind. They are separating from parents, finding their own centers. The Four Principles of Peace may take on a different meaning during these years.

· Redouble your efforts to listen deeply and to provide for the safe expression of feelings. As important as these are with younger children, they are doubly so with teens.

· Make sure teens have a safe space where they can talk about the pressures they feel to conform with the values of popular culture. These pressures can be a form of violence against the natural self, and can even lead to harmful and destructive behavior. Young people need adult confidantes and mentors—often outside the family—with whom they can explore these tensions in a trusting environment.

· While a culture of peace may not be forefront in their minds, remind teens about the Four Principles for Peace, and use them as standards by which the young people can assess some of the hard choices they face.

· Work with parents, teachers, and youth leaders to set up age-appropriate programs that provide alternatives to the violence so widespread in the popular culture.

· Get teens involved in the peace education of younger kids. Ask them to help set up new peace corners, to consult on teaching ideas and field trips for peace studies, to serve as mediators.

27 EMPOWER THE CHILDREN

Power and influence are important for everyone, regardless of age. Kids are learning about power from their earliest days. At first, because they are small and helpless, they learn that adults have power and they don't. They begin early on to find ways to exert influence on their environment. If they cannot find positive ways to do this, they will find negative ways.

Children are an essential part of our family and community life. They need to have a meaningful voice at home and school in the decisions that affect their lives. To be able to honor the Four Principles of Peace, children need to have the experience of being empowered to speak, to choose, and to question.

• Invite children into family discussions. Invite their participation in conversations about family matters large and small, from family outings to vacations, from house cleaning to house moving. Do the same in school classrooms and other settings where kids and adults live, work, and play together.

• Be clear about who makes which decisions. Where the decisions rest with the adults, make sure children know their opinions are being considered. Where the decisions are by consensus, have a process for reaching agreement. Having regular family or classroom meetings ensures that group conversation and decision making become an accepted way of being together.

• Ask young people to participate in creating rituals for resolving conflicts in the family, class, or group. Give them meaningful roles to play in these rituals, so they can be active in helping the group find its harmony again.

• Encourage ongoing conversation about the Four Principles of Peace, and ask children to design with you some creative ways they might be practiced in your home, school, or group setting.

REVIEW

Practice the Four Principles of Peace with Children

COMMUNITY
Relate to the natural selves of the children in your life, and help
them stay connected to that place in themselves and each other.

COOPERATION
Work together with parents, teachers, kids, and others
to promote alternatives to violence in popular culture.

NONVIOLENCE
Create norms for nonviolent family and school life, such
as peace corners, peer mediation, and family meetings.

WITNESS
Be steadfast in your commitment to raise
a new generation of peacekeepers.

BULLY BEGONE!

Children in many of our school systems are learning how to resolve their own conflicts without the intervention of an adult. Peer mediation, conflict resolution, and bullying-awareness programs have been proven effective in reducing violence at school and empowering children in the art of playground diplomacy. In this story, one elementary school teacher had the chance to see the direct benefits of her school's anti-bullying campaign.

I was on playground duty one day and saw Phoebe, age seven, take a big risk. She saw several second-grade boys ganging up on two kindergarten kids. At first, she told me later, she didn't want to get involved, because she was afraid the boys would turn on her if she said anything. Then she remembered the talk her class had had with the school counselor about bullying.

She went up to the group and stood in front of her classmates. "Hey," she said, "just think how these little kids feel when you make fun of them. They're only five years old! You're so much bigger than them— you're scaring them. Remember how it feels when the sixth graders gang up on you?"

The boys backed off without complaint. I went up to Phoebe and congratulated her on standing up to the bullies. She smiled shyly, with pleasure. "It wasn't so scary," she said. "I just did what Mrs. Jones taught us to do, and it worked!"

RESOURCE GUIDE

PROGRAMS AND ORGANIZATIONS

Check within your local community for programs on peer mediation, conflict resoltion in the schools, or nonviolent alternatives for youth. Here are some suggestions:

CHILDREN'S CREATIVE RESPONSE TO CONFLICT (CCRC)

Helps educators, parents, and those who work with young people learn creative skills of nonviolent conflict resolution through cooperation, communication, affirmation, problem solving, mediation, and bias awareness. Resources, staff, and student training workshops available.

NYACK, NY; PHONE: 914-353-1796; FAX: 914-358-4924;
E-MAIL: CCRCNYACK@aol.com;
WEB SITE: www.planet-rockland.org/conflict

EDUCATORS FOR SOCIAL RESPONSIBILITY

Seeks to make teaching social responsibility a core practice in education so that young people develop the convictions and skills needed to shape a safe, sustainable, democratic, and just world.

CAMBRIDGE, MA; PHONE: 617-492-1764 or 800-370-2515; FAX: 617-864-5164;
E-MAIL: educators@esrnational.org; WEB SITE: www.esrnational.org

THE LION AND LAMB PROJECT

Seeks to stop the marketing of violence to children by helping parents, industry, and government officials recognize that violence is not child's play, and by galvanizing concerned adults to take action. Works to reduce the marketing of violent toys, games, and entertainment to children.

BETHESDA, MD; PHONE: 301-654-3091; FAX: 301-718-8192;
E-MAIL: lionlamb@lionlamb.org; WEB SITE: www.lionlamb.org

THE PROGRAM FOR YOUNG NEGOTIATORS

Aims to build the capacity of young people, their teachers, and other mentors to use negotiation skills as a powerful means of achieving their goals. Promotes the use of collaboration, positive communication, and joint problem solving, and fosters an environment in which people constructively work through differences and adversity. Curriculum and training available.

CAMBRIDGE, MA; PHONE: 617-225-7877; FAX: 617-225-0027;
WEB SITE: www.pyn.org

BOOKS, TAPES, VIDEOS

Creative Conflict Resolution: More Than 200 Activities for Keeping Peace in the Classroom. William J. Kreidler. Goodyear, 1984.

Free the Children: Conflict Education for Strong, Peaceful Minds. Susan Gingras Fitzell, M.Ed. New Society, 1997.

One Day in Peace (a picture book in 21 languages). Steve Diamond and Robert Alan Silverstein. Illustrated by Ginger Nielson. 1996–2000. Free print out available online at *http://www.oneday.net.*

Waging Peace in Our Schools. Linda Lantieri, Janet Patti, and Marian Wright Edelman. Beacon Press, 1998.

WEB SITES

MAKE THE PEACE CAMPAIGN

Special tools for schools and youth for taking responsibility for making peace.

www.makethepeace.org

PEACELINKS

A program on this site, Youth Links = Safe Schools, is based on the premise that youth have the seeds of solutions to their own safety. Site offers resources and contact information.

www.peacelinks.org, click Youth Links

CONFLICT RESOLUTION EDUCATION NETWORK

Offers fact sheets on various aspects of conflict resolution education and peer mediation.

www.crenet.org

YOUTH PEACE

A War Resisters League campaign integrating work against war toys and military recruiting with developing a culture of nonviolence, beginning with our children.

www.warresisters.org, click Youth Peace Site

Keywords to explore through your computer search engine: *peace, peace education, nonviolence and children, peer mediation*

FOUR

PEACE AT WORK
A New Way of Doing Business

Work is love made visible.
—KAHLIL GIBRAN

———————

The workplace is the ideal setting in which to develop a culture of peace. We spend a major part of our lives at work, interacting with colleagues, bosses, customers, clients, and vendors. In many business environments, fierce competition, power struggles, and personality conflicts are the order of the day. It doesn't have to be that way.

The economy plays a big role, locally and globally, in matters of conflict and peace. How we gather and use our natural resources, what we produce in the way of goods and services, and how we distribute the results of our efforts (money, products, recognition) are all places where we can choose whether or not to practice the Four Principles of Peace.

Whatever our role—wage earner, volunteer, or temporary help; entrepreneur, manager, or corporate leader—we all can influence the culture of our work life. If we are not the decision makers, we can make suggestions, model the behaviors and values we desire, and let people know what's important to us. If we are the decision makers, we can set the tone and focus for a culture of peace.

28 PUT YOUR VALUES TO WORK

Peace at work begins with our values. Whether we are flipping burgers to get by or engaged in our most passionate life's calling, our hopes and dreams affect the culture we work in.

What is our vision for the work that we do? What do we want to accomplish? How will that achievement benefit us, our families, others? What are the values that affect where and how we work, who we work with, and what we work toward? These questions are meaningful whether we are answering phones, mopping floors, or negotiating multimillion-dollar deals. When we operate from this base, we can set our work life on a path of peace.

· Find out if your company or organization has a published mission or vision statement. Do you agree with it? Did you help create it? How would you change it if you could? What are you doing to support it? If such a statement does not exist, consider helping to write one.

· Ask yourself what is important to you about your work life. What values do you want to express through what you do? Talk with your colleagues at work about these values. Are they commonly shared? Is there a written set of operating values for your workplace? If not, consider helping create one.

· Consider an average day at your workplace. Ask yourself, "What did I do today that helped bring my vision a little closer to reality? What can I do tomorrow?"

· Consider one common and repeated activity in your work. Ask yourself, "How is this activity related to one or more of my basic values? How might I express even more strongly what I believe in through this activity?"

29   TURN POWER STRUGGLES INTO POWER SURGES

Power struggles are common in the workplace. With colleagues, between bosses and workers, across departments, or with competitors, we often battle to gain power and influence.

Power struggles can do great harm. If not managed early, they can easily escalate into more destructive conflict, poisoning the work atmosphere and hurting the bottom line of business success. Our productivity and our sense of joy in a job well done can be held hostage to a self-centered competition for place and prominence.

We need to understand the true nature of power. Real power is creative energy. It is available equally to everyone. We can pit our energies against each other, seeking personal advantage or control (power "over"), or we can put our energies together toward a shared goal (power "with"), creating a power surge.

• Change the direction of your power. Imagine having power over someone at work; now imagine having power with them. Imagine going nose to nose with someone; now imagine joining hip to hip, to face a shared problem together. What do you notice?

• Work from the inside out. If you find yourself in a power struggle at work, take a moment to reconnect with your natural self (through the various techniques mentioned in earlier chapters). From this place of inner peace, consider what you might have in common with this other person and how you can build fruitfully on that common ground. Then do it.

• Help mediate power disputes. If there is a power struggle going on in your workplace that doesn't involve you directly, consider inviting the parties to sit down with you to discuss how they might redirect all that energy into a more cooperative approach.

30   HONOR DIVERSITY AT WORK

The variety of the human family is its strength. We have many differences: of race, ethnicity, gender, age, religion, sexual orientation. This diversity—and the tensions and prejudices often associated with it—can enrich or destroy our work culture, depending on how well we respect and appreciate each other.

The biggest differences are related to identity, a critical element of our human experience. Everyone wants their identity recognized. Everyone wants to be treated equally and with respect. Everyone wants to know that they can be who they are, without negative reactions from others.

- Notice your prejudices. We all carry thoughts and feelings about people's different identities. We naturally absorb these views from our social environment. Becoming aware of how our assumptions feed negative stereotyping, we can begin to replace them with more positive, respectful thoughts.

- Be sensitive to the legacy of hurt. Many of us may have experienced personal discrimination, or "our people" may have suffered harm because of who they were. This pain makes us especially vulnerable to even casual slights or signs of disrespect, especially in matters of hiring, firing, and promotions. Be aware of your own legacy of pain, and those of others, so you can reduce the risk of increasing the hurt.

- Practice curiosity. Find someone at work whose identity is different from yours in some significant way. Reach out to them with an attitude of nonjudgmental interest. Learn about their culture and their history. Ask about their holidays, food, and customs. Discover areas of commonality despite differences.

- Know what is important to you about your own identity. We often take our identity for granted—it's "normal" for us, and everyone else is different. We forget that to others, we're the ones who are different. What aspects of your identity might you share at work to widen the perspective of others?

31   ENJOY TEAMWORK

Teamwork is the perfect learning laboratory for the Four Principles of Peace. Working together toward a single goal, each team member must go beyond his or her personal ego and work for the good of the whole. Teamwork builds trust and offers avenues for personal and collective success. This is a recipe for peace.

Many people learn the joys of teamwork through sports activities. That same sense of excitement and camaraderie can happen in the workplace, without the element of competition. By pooling our resources and sharing a common goal, we can achieve greater results and have more fun in the process.

• Join teams. If you are in a position to organize how others work, assign teams to specific projects. If your boss doesn't assign you to a team, create one on your own. The best teammates are not always the people most alike; make sure your teams have people who bring very different skills and views to the group, for good cross-fertilization.

• Promote creativity. The old saying, "Two heads are better than one," applies to good teamwork. Freeing up the creative juices of all team members brings new ideas and fresh approaches. Use brainstorming, or creative thinking sessions, to put more possibilities on the table.

• Aim for high performance. Members of a high-performance team are less interested in their personal ego satisfaction than in the achievements of the whole. It means sharing, not withholding, all your resources. It means focusing your energies in the same direction for a joint success.

• Get help in developing good teamwork. Teamwork doesn't necessarily come naturally for everyone. Specialists in teamwork can provide short and useful training in how to work effectively as a team.

32 CREATE A NOURISHING ORGANIZATIONAL CULTURE

Creating a product or delivering a service is only one part of the work equation. Our work must also feed us as human beings. We get this nourishment from the experience of being at work as well as from the tasks we accomplish. The process is as important as the product.

Organizational culture is the set of often unwritten expectations that determine how we treat each other in the workplace. When that culture is open, trusting, and embracing, we are happy to be at work and will more readily participate with all Four Principles of Peace in the workplace.

• Set clear boundaries for proper workplace behavior. No one wants to be harassed, intimidated, insulted, taken advantage of, or violated by anyone at work. Encourage your organization to make clear rules about these things, and to honor and enforce them.

• Let every voice be heard. We all want to feel included. Everyone, from the lowliest position to the highest management, has an opinion to offer about how the work might go better. Step forward with your own ideas, and encourage others to do the same.

• Appreciate, appreciate, appreciate. When people feel appreciated, they participate more fully. We all want our gifts acknowledged, our value recognized. We can appreciate our colleagues formally (through awards, raises, and extra benefits) or informally, through saying, "Thanks," or acknowledging a job well done. This is also the heart of good customer service.

• Grow through work. When our work is boring, we withdraw our resources. When our work challenges us and gives us the opportunity to develop new skills, we work more enthusiastically. We can encourage each other to stretch beyond our limits, for our own good and the good of the organization.

33   PRACTICE SHARED RESPONSIBILITY

Everyone has a stake in the success of their work situation. Everyone can be a leader of some kind. If all the members of a business are sharing a sense of responsibility for the whole, the company will be stronger, and the culture of peace will thrive.

• Empower yourself and others. Some decisions need approval from supervisors, but the more people can exercise their own decision-making ability, the more they are able to work effectively and cooperatively.

• Find opportunities to practice and share leadership. Meetings and presentations do not always have to be headed by the same people. Managing special projects, leading a team effort, or being responsible for the completion of a particular task—no matter how small—can build a sense of commitment and inclusion.

• Take the initiative. If you want to try something new, go for it. If you see something that needs to happen, make it happen. If you have an idea, put it forward. Demonstrate that you feel responsible for the whole through your actions.

• Consider shared ownership. Many companies have found they can increase productivity and participation by including their staff in some mechanism of ownership, such as stock options, co-ownership plans, or commissions. When we share ownership, we are strengthening the web of peace, for then we all become responsible for each other.

34 HAVE A PROCESS FOR CONFLICT RESOLUTION

Since differences are natural, some conflict in the workplace is inevitable. If we establish a clear process by which these disputes can be worked out successfully before they escalate, we keep the center of peace at work.

• Use formal and informal processes. Many companies have formal grievance procedures. These are important, but equally important are the informal processes through which disagreements can be worked out before they need to go through formal channels.

• Identify in-house mediators. There are some people who are naturally good at helping other people solve their problems together. They are trustworthy, respected, clear-headed, and a stable and peaceful presence. Identify these people, and train them as mediators or troubleshooters, impartial third parties to whom others can feel comfortable taking their disputes.

• Use outside consultants. Often a staff or team will develop patterns of conflict that need additional help in resolving or changing. Bringing in an outside facilitator or mediator can not only help unravel the knots, but it can also present opportunities for everyone to increase their skill in conflict resolution.

• Make conflict resolution normative. Set the tone that conflict is natural and is an opportunity to learn and grow and be more successful as a business. Encourage the use of the processes that have been set up to resolve differences. Appreciate and reward those who use these processes appropriately.

35 SEE WORK AS SERVICE

We all want to feel that our lives and our actions are making some contribution to the larger good. This motivation to service can inspire and infuse the workplace, whatever the nature of our work might be.

It is not just the so-called service industry that provides a service to the community. Whether we are producing widgets, computers, or light bulbs, whether we are giving nursing care, cooking meals, or teaching children, we are making a contribution. The more we see and acknowledge that contribution, the more we are joining the larger culture of peace.

• Make "work as service" part of the conversation. Discuss at staff meetings or other settings how the business is of service to the immediate or larger community, and how it could be even more so.

• Give something back. Find a way to interact with your community, to show appreciation and make a contribution for the greater good: have a public picnic, run a food or toy drive, host an open-house tour of your company, give free samples, support a local public health campaign, make a financial donation to a worthy local cause—the possibilities are endless.

• Push for a policy of community service as part of work time. In some companies, staff can use work time to be of service to the community. Do some research into this, and consider adopting or adapting it as a policy in your work setting.

• Work for peace. Consider starting, working for, or partnering with a business whose work is specifically related to peace. Find ways for your organization to make a tangible contribution to building a culture of peace: for instance, dedicate some percentage of your profits to peace-related activities, sponsor a public affairs essay contest, or host a citizen exchange program event.

36   BE SOCIALLY RESPONSIBLE AT WORK

Because of our interconnectedness, our work—whatever it may be—will have an impact on the people and places around us, near and far. We cannot ignore these effects—we must acknowledge them and take responsibility for them. From a practical point of view, from a moral perspective, and in the interest of short-term and long-term peace and well-being, this is important.

• Consider the ethical impact of your work. If you make a mess, clean it up. If your work causes harm to anyone, find ways to do it harmlessly—and help heal the hurt you have caused. If your work depletes a shared resource, fill up the pot again. If you take, give back.

• Assess the social impact of your work. How does your business touch the lives of its customers, vendors, suppliers? What about the people in the community where you work? Does it enrich their lives, or does it deplete them? Are you taking unfair advantage of some need in order to get low prices? Are you pushing the edge of legal and ethical behavior? Make these questions part of the ongoing conversation at your workplace, and take whatever action necessary to promote a healthy and responsible relationship with your larger community.

• Consider the environmental impact of your work. What natural resources are you using? What by-products do you return to the air, the water, the Earth? Take concrete action to ensure your company walks lightly on the Earth, leaving the natural world as clean and healthy a legacy for our children as possible.

• Also assess the personal impact of your work. Burnout, boredom, constant tension, and failure will drag down the individual and the company. Take time during the day to recharge your batteries through a variety of self-care approaches (exercise, stretching, good nutrition, massage). Help others do the same.

REVIEW

Practice the Four Principles of Peace at Work

COMMUNITY
Have an organizational vision and culture that benefits all involved.

COOPERATION
Honor diversity, show appreciation, practice
teamwork, and share responsibility.

NONVIOLENCE
Encourage informal and formal conflict resolution processes.

WITNESS
Live peace by giving the highest ethical value
to the social and environmental impact of your work.

THE BUSINESS OF PEACE

Some companies are supporting peace by bringing people together across conflict lines for mutual economic benefit. In the following case, the company owner became extremely discouraged after violence flared in the Middle East, where he had an important project. His project partners, however, reminded him of the need for perserverance.

Many years ago, when things were starting to take off in my business and my Israeli and Palestinian partners were working well together, a terrorist bomb went off in Tel Aviv, killing many people.

I was disquieted and depressed. I felt powerless and questioned what I was doing. "I'm trying to bring people together through work, and one terrorist takes it upon himself to blow up sixty people. . . . It's just a waste of time to make this large effort when this is happening. Who I am kidding, to believe I can make a difference, when people are being blown up?"

In that frame of mind, I called my two local partners, one Israeli Jewish and one Palestinian Israeli, and said I was thinking about closing shop; that I couldn't continue talking about peace through tomatoes when people were dying.

"Are you crazy?" they answered. "We are the ones on the front lines, and we're not giving up! This is our livelihood. We cannot stop this because someone is trying to stop the peace process. We won't be hostages to that. We don't have that alternative, to give up. This is how we put food on the table."

Their response opened my eyes, and re-energized me. Once you take this path, there's no going back. Lack of co-existence, of interaction, is not an option. When so-called enemies work together, it really humanizes the situation. Plus it creates a powerful economic bond—their liveilihoods are tied together, their success depends on each other.

N.B.: The outbreak of intense Israeli-Palestinian violence in the fall of 2000 made it extremely difficult for Israelis and Palestinians to cooperate in projects such as this. The company owner, though sad, has not lost his conviction that business and peace go together.

RESOURCE GUIDE

Check in your local community for programs related to conflict resolution, ethics, or social responsibility in the workplace. Here are some suggestions:

PROGRAMS AND ORGANIZATIONS

BUSINESS FOR SOCIAL RESPONSIBILITY

A membership organization for companies of all sizes and sectors whose mission is to help companies be commercially successful while demonstrating respect for ethical values, people, communities and the environment.

SAN FRANCISCO, CA; PHONE: 415-537-0888; FAX: 415-537-0889;
WEB SITE: www.bsr.org

PEACE CEREAL

Peace Cereal's mission is to serve you by making deliciously natural and healthy cereal, as well as to serve the world community by utilizing responsible business practices and donating 10% of our profits to peace.

EUGENE, OR; PHONE: 800-964-4832 ; FAX: 541-461-2191;
E-MAIL: INFO@PEACECEREAL.COM; WEB SITE: www.peacecereal.com

PeaceWorks

Uses business as a driving force for bringing together divided rivals in viable enterprises, simultaneously laying the practical groundwork for reconciliation.

NEW YORK, NY; PHONE: 212-616-3006; FAX: 212-616-3005;
E-MAIL: info@peaceworks.net; WEB SITE: www.peaceworks.com

PROGRAM ON NEGOTIATION
SENIOR EXECUTIVE SEMINARS

Harvard University Law School's Program on Negotiation offers special training programs for improving negotiation skills in the workplace, including increasing human resource effectiveness, negotiating labor agreements, and managing international business relationships.

WELLESLEY, MA; PHONE: 781-239-1111; FAX: 781-239-1546;
E-MAIL: info@pon.execseminars.com ;
WEB SITE: www.pon.execseminars.com

BOOKS, TAPES, VIDEOS

Building a House for Diversity: A Fable about a Giraffe and an Elephant Offers New Strategies for Today's Workforce. R. Roosevelt Thomas, Jr., with Marjorie I. Woodruff, 1999.

Getting to Yes: Negotiating Agreements Without Giving In. Roger Fisher, William Ury, and Bruce Patton. Penguin USA, 1991.

The Natural Step for Business: Wealth, Ecology, and the Evolutionary Corporation. Brian Nattrass, Mary Altomare, and Brian Naijrass. New Society, 1999.

Six Roles for Business in Peacebuilding. Louise Diamond, IMTD Occasional Paper Series, available from IMTD: 703-528-3863 or imtd@imtd.org.

WEB SITES

BUSINESS LEADERS FOR SENSIBLE PRIORITIES

Initiative of business leaders to support the wise investment of U.S. tax dollars, balancing domestic, international, and military needs.
www.commondreams.org

MAKE THE PEACE CAMPAIGN

Offers practical suggestions for peace in the workplace.
www.angelfire.com/mn/makethepeace/mtp3.html

WWW.MEDIATE.COM

Resources and training for conflict resolution, mediation, and arbitration in the workplace.
www.mediate.com/workplace

FIVE

PEACE & PUBLIC AFFAIRS
Building the Peace-Able Community

*Never doubt that a small group of dedicated people can
change the world. Indeed, it is the only thing that ever has.*
—MARGARET MEAD

———————

We all live in community. Our personal, family, and work lives are part of that larger context. We are surrounded by neighbors and strangers who, like us, are concerned about everyday matters that affect us all—matters relating to education, environment, health care, housing, land use, taxes, and so on.

As we grapple with these issues at the local and national levels, we find many opportunities for conflict or for peace. Rubbing up against each other with the great variety of our experiences, opinions, and interests, we are constantly defining and redefining our community's culture and the quality of life for all its members.

Applying the Four Principles of Peace in our community life allows us to be conscious about creating, together, the kind of public environment we want for ourselves and for our children. It allows us to build the Peace-able Community—a community that has committed itself to right relationship based on justice, dignity, respect, and nonviolence.

37   JOIN THE PUBLIC CONVERSATION

We need to talk to each other about the matters that matter in our lives. Whether the issue is gun control or classroom size, the nearby sewage treatment plant or the homeless, fishing rights or election finance reform—the issues that touch our collective lives require a collective conversation.

Our conversation needs to be broad and inclusive. It needs to be civil and respectful of differences. It needs to be specific and ultimately lead to consensus and action. But most of all, it needs to be public. That is, people need to join in, listen, and be heard. Without wide participation, the conversation is limited to those most passionately for or against, which leads to polarization, animosity, and stalemate.

• Identify a public affairs issue that affects your life. Perhaps it touches you or your family directly, or perhaps it touches your heart or your sense of fairness.

• Do some research. Find information on the issue that supports a variety of views. What have other communities done on this issue? What has worked? What has not been successful?

• Go to public meetings. Watch local papers or listen to the radio for open meetings on this subject. Perhaps your city council will discuss it, or a church or synagogue group, or a public affairs organization.

• Join the media discussion. Public conversations are happening all the time through the media. Call in to talk radio shows; read and write letters to the editor in local papers and national magazines; join online chat rooms on the Internet.

• Create a forum for discussion. Call a meeting, start a study group, invite neighbors in for coffee and conversation, begin a dialogue session. Get people talking to one another any way you can.

38 START WHERE YOU ARE

When you join a larger conversation, it is helpful to know your point of reference, where you begin from. What are your own views on the subject? Are they already well formed? Are you open to learning more? How flexible are you about the subject? Is there room for change in your mind?

Think of your participation in a public affairs conversation as an opportunity to learn and grow and to make a difference. It is a place to practice all Four Principles of Peace, affirming that we are, indeed, all in this together and can move with cooperation and respect to solve—without violence—the most difficult challenges of our shared community life.

- Begin with values. Ask yourself what is really important to you about this issue. What values, ideals, or hopes are the basis for your views? What higher goal or vision can be served?

- Uncover your assumptions. Your views are fed by underlying beliefs and attitudes. What are they? What do you assume to be true regarding this issue you have chosen to get involved with? Search for the unspoken, invisible convictions you carry, perhaps without even knowing it.

- Distinguish emotions from opinions. Emotions are feeling states; opinions are thoughts we have about something. What opinions do you have about the subject you have chosen? How does the subject touch your emotions—what do you feel about it?

- Consider possible solutions. Have you reached a conclusion about action that could or should be taken to resolve the issue? What are the solutions you would propose? How attached are you to them? Can you let go and make room for an entirely new set of options?

39 DIALOGUE TO UNDERSTAND

A healthy conversation moves from personal awareness to dialogue. Our tendency is to rush to action, to try to "fix" the problem. Yet, without full understanding of the issues and the various viewpoints, any agreement for action is likely to be premature.

Our first goal, then, is understanding. We need to learn what's important about this matter to the people who are engaged in the conversation. We need to explore what might be under the surface of the visible conversation. What emotions, hopes, fears, history, or needs lie beneath the tip of the iceberg? How are they driving the discussion? This is the time to collect information.

• Distinguish dialogue from debate. A debate is about proving a point. It has winners and losers. Dialogue is about mutual understanding and learning together. Helping others realize this difference can greatly improve the quality of the public conversation.

• Be curious. Approach different views with the wonder and awe of a child. Why would someone think in that way? How did they get to that view? How does it make sense to them? Even, and especially, if it doesn't make sense to you.

• Share assumptions. If the conversation stays at the level of opinion and never considers the assumptions beneath those views, it will not get very far. Express your own assumptions as you realize them, and make it safe and normal for others to do the same.

• Welcome the stories. We make sense of our lives through story. We tell ourselves stories about what happened to us, or what could happen. If we listen closely, we realize that these stories contain our basic assumptions, values, and feelings. We can change our story when we get new information. Invite people to tell their stories; tell your own.

40   SEEK COMMON GROUND AND CONSENSUS

Many of our public conversations are highly emotional and adversarial. This is because they relate to issues that are very important to us ideologically, emotionally, or physically.

The Four Principles of Peace suggest that we bring a different tone to the conversation, one that helps us discover the points of common interest within our diverse views. Finding our common ground gives us a strong foundation for successful action.

• Hold consensus as a goal. Consensus does not mean everyone has to agree. It does mean everyone can find enough to agree on that they are willing to go along with a particular decision. Keep telling yourself, and others, that consensus is possible, even in the most heated debates.

• Resist the urge to argue. When discussing hot topics, we want to jump in and argue when we hear opinions we strongly disagree with. Argument begets more argument, and reduces the chance for consensus. Put the urge aside, and find a more inviting way to speak your piece.

• List the points of agreements. Listen for the areas where there is overlapping interest, joint concern, and commonly held views. Make note of them, and report them back into the larger conversation, so everyone involved can notice what the common ground is.

• Check for consensus. From time to time, check back with the group in conversation to see if you have reached consensus. "It seems like we're in basic agreement on this—is that true?" When you have consensus on one subject, move on to the next.

41 ADDRESS NEEDS AND INTERESTS RATHER THAN POSITIONS

As the dialogue moves past understanding toward resolution, it helps to be able to sort out the positions from the interests and to know the basic needs that are behind it all.

Positions are stands we take, strongly, for our preferred way to address an issue. Interests are the things that matter to us about the issue, what's important to us that leads us to take the position we do. Needs are the basic human requirements that we all share for safety and survival, for belonging and growth. Needs can be met; interests can be satisfied through negotiation, but positions are usually mutually exclusive and invite polarization and heightened conflict.

• Practice distinguishing positions, interests, and needs. Listen to your own views first and see if you can say what your position is, what the underlying interests are, and what are the basic needs at the core. Do the same for the different parties in the conversation.

• Repeat the interests of the other side. Showing that you really heard what's important to others by repeating back to them their interests can be a great benefit to the conversation. Everyone wants to know they've been heard.

• Find common needs. We all have the same basic needs, and these needs are intertwined. My need for feeling safe is more likely to be met if you also feel safe. If you feel welcome and honored, you are more likely to extend the same to me. See if you can identify—and act on—the shared needs of all parties to the discussion.

• Think of ways to satisfy the interests of all parties. Knowing the interests allows us to consider options for satisfying them. Be creative in coming up with options. See how many you can list when you put your heads together as a group. Select from the whole list one or two ideas that might be most successful as an action step. Then do them.

42   GET HELP FROM THIRD PARTIES

Sometimes the discussion of public issues gets stuck. We end up in a stalemate of opposing views, full of negative feelings and growing hostility. We need to call for help.

There is a whole profession of people who are trained to act as third parties to difficult conversations. A third party is someone who is not involved in the dispute, who can be an impartial guide to the process. This can take various forms: it might be someone who facilitates or manages the conversation so that it is more fruitful, or someone who actually mediates the dispute to help arrive at consensus for action.

• Find local resources. Many lawyers, organizational consultants, and human behavior specialists offer services as facilitators or mediators for community issues. Look in the Yellow Pages under "Mediation Services" or online at *www.mediate.com*. Ask around for personal references.

• Involve others in engaging a third party. Find other people active in the conversation to work with you in securing the services of a third party. Seek especially those whose opinions differ from yours, so that the suggestion of using a third party is not associated with any one point of view.

• Learn from the process. Participate in the facilitated or mediated sessions fully, and at the same time see what you can learn about the process of third-party help. You can use any skills you pick up in further conversations, when the third party is no longer present.

• Consider getting trained yourself in facilitation or mediation skills. If you find the process useful, you might want to improve your ability to use these methods. Many third parties offer training programs or know where you can find them.

43 TURN ENEMIES INTO ALLIES

Our public policy conversations can be extremely confrontational. Emotions run high; positions get hardened; name calling overtakes civility; and people begin to see those who hold different views as their opponents or enemies.

When we see each other as enemies, we are in battle. This robs us all of our individual and communal peace. We need to think about how the Four Principles of Peace can prevent us getting to this state, or, if we are already there, how they can help us bring peace back to the situation.

• Be grateful to those with opposing views. See what you can learn from them. Their different perspective is one of many voices that make up the whole; yours is another. Without their ideas, you would have nothing to push against to grow and develop.

• Make personal contact. Even with our bitterest opponents we can find something in common. Maybe we both have children or like the same kind of ice cream. Reaching out in this way says that the person is not the problem; that even if we disagree, we can have a friendly relationship.

• Refuse to do battle. Don't attack the people who disagree with you, and if you are attacked, make clear that this isn't about personalities but about the issue. Refuse to participate in blaming, name calling, or making demeaning statements about others.

· See the problem as a shared opportunity. The issue is not the people; the issue is out there somewhere, where you can both stand together and look at it. Invite your so-called opponents to work with you rather than against you to address the real issues under discussion; allies in a larger struggle benefit the whole community.

· Act from your own place of inner peace. Go home to your center, breathe, and relax. Keep your heart and mind open.

44 BUILD BRIDGES AND ALLIANCES

Being effective on matters of public policy requires collective action. Your own involvement is a good first step. Next, it's important to make the connections that can take action to a broader level.

The act of building bridges, networks, coalitions, and alliances is more than a way to get things done. It's a way of creating an infra-structure so that the public conversation about community affairs can be grounded in action. It is also a practical demonstration of the Four Principles of Peace.

· Talk to your friends about your involvement in public affairs dialogue. Share your enthusiasm and your concerns. Invite them to join you.

· Discover existing networks. Many critical issues in our public life are already served by various organizations, publications, and structured activities. Tap into what already exists, bringing your resources with you.

· Offer to be an information bridge. Sometimes different groups are working on similar issues but don't know what the other is doing. You can build a link by sharing that information back and forth. Or, you can host regular gatherings where everyone involved can share information on their activities.

· Create formal structures. Organize a Steering Committee, a Task Force, a Partnership Project—structures that bring various individuals and groups together on a common topic. Give the structure a name, a clear task, a small budget, and assignments for action.

· Create informal structures. Bring people together for one-time meetings, for short-term activities, for informational exchanges. Let the process evolve on its own from there.

45   REFUSE TO SUPPORT AN ADVERSARIAL APPROACH

The conversations about many of our critical public affairs issues are currently being conducted in a combat mode. The issues are presented in terms of black and white, right and wrong; you are either "for" or "'against." People with differing views align themselves in "camps" and adopt a fighting posture against those in other camps.

Politicians—local and national—and other community leaders encourage this polarization. They use their political platforms to turn up the heat on issues central to their election campaigns or political identity. They present issues simplistically and narrowly, and make negative statements about their political opponents who hold other views.

· Speak out. By keeping silent on this strategy, we allow it to continue. We need to actively say "No" to polarization and "Yes" to civility in dialogue.

· Promote dialogue. The culture of dialogue is an antidote to the culture of polarization. Dialogue brings people together to find common cause; polarization keeps people apart to continue the battle.

· Use the power of your vote. Let your political representatives know that you do not appreciate statements and approaches that demean others; that you consider uncivil public discourse an unacceptable form of violence. Vote in other leaders who have demonstrated a "We're all in this together" approach.

· Demonstrate your successes. The negative mode is familiar to people, and to leaders, because they are ignorant about other possibilities. When you have a successful example of a civil civic conversation that was able to build consensus for action, publicize it. Show people how it can look when done right.

REVIEW

Practice the Four Principles of Peace and Public Affairs

COMMUNITY
Be a builder of networks and bridges
for a broader impact on public affairs.

COOPERATION
Work together, rather than against
each other, for joint problem solving.

NONVIOLENCE
Practice civility in public discourse;
refuse to support polarizing debate.

WITNESS
Engage in dialogue from a place of inner peace,
honoring the values, opinions, and feelings of all parties.

FROM DEBATE TO DIALOGUE

Many towns and cities, at some time, will face issues that threaten to divide and polarize the community. How we deal with these issues determines whether we tear apart our social fabric or find ways to build bridges and consensus. This story shows how one community started down the path of polarization but pulled itself back in time to rediscover a sense of common civic pride.

My town was deeply divided over the issue of a pedestrian mall for our aging Main Street. Sides rapidly chose up, and when some out-of-state developers joined the conversation, it became a rancorous debate.

Each side thought the other was naive at best, mean-spirited at worst. Words like *stupid* and *greedy* were thrown around. "Celebrate Main Street" and "Don't Fall for the Mall" showed up on posters and bumper stickers all around town.

The city council sponsored a series of public meetings. The first was a disaster—it ended just short of a full-fledged brawl. The council hired a professional facilitator to manage the next two meetings. She did a good job of making sure that everyone had a voice and was listened to with respect. For the first time, the mall supporters were able to hear how afraid the merchants were that the influx of national chain stores would put them out of business and destroy a unique spirit of community. The mall opponents, who preferred the option of paint, polish, and beautification, were able to hear the results of independent studies showing the success of pedestrian malls elsewhere.

The issue is still under discussion, with no decisions made as yet. However, the posters have come down, and the outlines of a consensus are starting to emerge: a smaller mall than was originally planned; a booster committee to support local businesses; plenty of benches and flower beds. Most important, the civility is back, and we feel like a community again.

RESOURCE GUIDE

Check within your local community for public affairs events and organizations and for mediators who can facilitate public conversations on difficult topics. Here are some suggestions:

PROGRAMS AND ORGANIZATIONS

CONSENSUS BUILDING INSTITUTE

Provides, encourages, and supports dispute resolution and consensus building on a worldwide basis. CBI provides dispute systems design, mediation of multiparty disputes, training, and a wide range of facilitation services, particularly in public disputes related to development, environmental protection, resource allocation, and peacemaking.

CAMBRIDGE, MA; PHONE: 617-492-1414; FAX: 617-492-1919; E-MAIL: consensus@cbuilding.org; WEB SITE: www.cbi-web.org

NATIONAL ASSOCIATION FOR COMMUNITY MEDIATION

A nonprofit organization of community mediation centers, staff, and volunteer mediators dedicated solely to community-based mediation programs. Offers members funding possibilities, research, publications, and more.

WASHINGTON, DC; PHONE: 202-667-9700; FAX: 202-667-8629; E-MAIL: lbaron@nafcm.org; WEB SITE: www.igc.org/nafcm

PUBLIC CONVERSATIONS PROJECT

Promotes constructive conversations and relationships among those whose conflicts about issues of public significance involve major differences in values and worldviews. PCP provides dialogue facilitation, training, consultation, presentations, and conference design for groups seeking to decrease polarization, increase mutual understanding, and open new possibilities for collaborative action.

WATERTOWN, MA; PHONE: 617-923-1216; FAX: 617-923-2757; E-MAIL: info@publicconversations.org; WEB SITE: www.publicconversations.org

BOOKS, TAPES, VIDEOS

The Consensus Building Handbook. Lawrence Susskind, editor. Sage Publications, 1999.

Starting a New Conversation When Debate Is Fruitless. Margaret Herzig. *Dispute Resolution* magazine (a publication of the American Bar Association), Summer 1998.

The Third Side: Why We Fight and How We Can Stop. William Ury. Penguin, 2000.

WEB SITES

MAKE THE PEACE CAMPAIGN

Offers practical suggestions for peace in the community.
www.angelfire.com/mn/makethepeace/mtp3.html

WWW.MEDIATE.COM

Resources and training for conflict resolution and mediation in the community.
www.mediate.com/community

THE THIRD SIDE

Resources and training for constructive conflict resolution.
www.thirdside.org

Keywords to explore through your computer search engine: *mediation, community mediation, community relations, consensus building*

SIX

PEACE & CO-EXISTENCE
Honoring Our Diversity

*I have a dream that my four children will one day
live in a nation where they will not be judged by the color
of their skin but by the content of their character.*
—REV. MARTIN LUTHER KING, JR.

The human family is wildly, delightfully diverse. We come in a huge variety of sizes, shapes, and colors. Our religions and belief systems, our cultures and traditions, our languages and lifestyles, even our geographical challenges and adaptations, are rich in their differences.

For whatever reason, these differences have become reasons to fight with each other or to claim superiority and power. We divide ourselves along the lines of our differences, seeing ourselves as the center of all that is good and right and everyone else as "the other." At their deepest, these divisions are expressed as racism, sexism, ageism, homophobia, xenophobia, and other rigid walls of hatred, discrimination, and fear.

If we're truly going to live at peace in our local and global communities, we need to get over these arbitrary divisions and learn to live together in harmony. We will have to remember that our unity as a single family of life on this Earth, and our wonderful diversity within that unity, are but two sides of the same coin. We are one, and we are many. When our intergroup relationships express this truth, we have laid a strong foundation for the culture of peace.

46 CELEBRATE THE DIFFERENCES

Anyone reading this right now who is a woman, stand up. If you are more than forty years old, stand up. If you are a Buddhist, stand up. If you are more than six feet tall, stand up.

Stand up if you are gay or lesbian. Stand up if you are of Asian heritage. If you speak Spanish, stand up. If you celebrate Kwanza, stand up. If you are of mixed racial or ethnic background, stand up. Stand up if you have never seen snow.

If you have completed high school, stand up. If you have children, stand up. Stand up if you are adopted. Stand up if you are not currently employed outside the home. Stand up if you earn more than $100,000 per year. If you believe in God, stand up. If you recycle your newspapers, stand up. If you would like to lose weight, stand up.

How many times did you stand up? Do you know at least one person who could stand up for each of these categories? Would you like to?

Each of these "categories" represents some of our differences as human beings. There are thousands, perhaps millions, of possible categories. Some of them are inherited traits that we cannot change; some are matters of choice and preference; some are more important to our sense of identity than others; some are very private matters.

You have a choice about how you relate to the people who didn't stand up when you did. You can see them as "other," or you can see them as like yourself but a little different. Maybe someone would not stand when you did on one question, but would on five others. When does that difference matter to you, and why?

If you would celebrate all the variety of who we are, start with yourself. Can you appreciate and honor your many selves—all the times you stood up, and the times you didn't? Now can you do that with others?

47   GO BEYOND STEREOTYPES AND PREJUDICES

A recent survey in the United States on views about the Middle East peace process showed that nearly 90 percent of respondents associated the word *terrorist* with the word *Arab.* This is an example of a vicious and prejudicial stereotype, a rigid perception that lumps everyone in a single group with a supposed common trait.

Our prejudices make it impossible for us to live together in peace, because they keep us from seeing each other as we really are. Because we live in a society where our differences separate us, we all carry distorted views of those with identities other than our own. Our work for peace is to learn to get beyond these distortions and see the beauty in each and every member of the human family.

- Pick one category mentioned in the exercise for which you did not stand up (or a category that was not mentioned at all) and about which you have strong feelings. List honestly your beliefs and assumptions about people in that category. Where did you learn those beliefs?

- Seek out some people of that category. Make an effort to get to know them as individuals, as real and complex human beings. (This takes courage, and maybe a bit of ingenuity to find them and make contact. You can do it.) What happens to the beliefs about them you started with?

- Pick one category in the exercise for which you did stand up, or one aspect of your identity of which you feel particularly proud. What stereotypes and prejudices do you think others may hold about people like you? To what extent are they true or not true about you? How might you re-educate those who hold these negative views?

48 PRACTICE CROSS-CULTURAL COMMUNICATION

Nearly every interaction we have with another person is some kind of cross-cultural communication. That is because our great diversity means that we have different beliefs, values, and assumptions. Even among men and women of the same ethnic group, age range, and religion, there can be enough distinction to require particular care in communicating.

Cross-cultural communication means that we take care to speak and act in ways that will not offend someone who is different from us, and that will ensure that what we say can be understood.

• Be sensitive to obvious differences of language, tradition, or religion. Be aware of words or actions that would clearly offend someone else (example: swearing in front of a devoutly religious person).

• Pay attention to the invisible differences that might make communication difficult. You cannot assume that people who look like you actually think like you. People have different expectations about time, touching, personal space, eye contact. What's comfortable for you may not be so for others.

• Take your cues from the other person. If they look you directly in the eye, you can probably safely do the same. If they shake hands, don't offer to hug. If they turn every personal question aside, don't keep asking.

• Be curious with people from cultures very different from your own. Admit your ignorance about their ways, and ask to be educated. Apologize in advance for any errors in etiquette you might make from your ignorance.

• Get the hint. If someone acts in a way that you consider strange or inappropriate, realize there may be significant cultural differences, rather than assume they are weird or stupid.

49 SEE YOURSELF AS THE OTHER

Often when we relate to people different than ourselves, we exaggerate the distinctions. We put all the "strangeness" in them, and all the "normalcy" in us. We need to be able to reach across that chasm and re-establish ourselves as sharing a common humanity.

We need to be able to look in the mirror and see the other as ourselves. We also need to be able to put ourselves in the shoes of the other, to understand how things look from their point of view.

• Think of another category of people whom you experience as "the other."

• Make a list of all the ways they are different from you. Now take each item on that list and apply it to yourself. See if it fits, even a little bit.

• Now make another list of all the ways they are the same as or similar to you. What do you notice?

• Set aside one hour of an average day in your life, and during that hour imagine that you are someone from that other category. How would your life be different in that hour?

• Think of a difficult situation you experienced or witnessed involving someone from an identity group different from yours. Tell the story of what happened. Now tell it from their likely point of view.

• Think of a story, myth, or legend that celebrates some victory of your group against another. How do you think people in that other group might feel when they hear your version of that victory? Now think of a story, myth, or legend that mourns a defeat of your group at the hands of another. How do you think the other group might tell this story to its children? What do you learn from this?

50   REBALANCE THE POWER EQUATION

In relationships between groups of people, usually one group has more power or privilege than another. Most power relations are based on an assumption of what is called a "zero-sum game." That means, if I have more, you must have less. Or they are acted out in a dominant-subordinate relationship, where the stronger side controls the weaker.

These formulas will always create tension and conflict, because generally people do not enjoy feeling "one down" while another is "one up." To build a culture of peace in our intergroup relations, we need to find creative ways for all to feel powerful.

- Think of a group that has more power (prestige or privilege) in society than a group you are associated with (example: men or women; adults or children; Protestants or Jews). Make a list of the ways that power is demonstrated.

- Think of a group that has less power (prestige or privilege) in society than a group you are associated with. Make a list of the ways that powerlessness is demonstrated.

- Now make a list of all the things that the more powerful group could do to equalize the power equation. What could the less powerful group do? How could this happen without creating greater conflict, or without reversing places so that the ones on top become the ones on the bottom?

- Think of situations you know about where the power balance was successfully restored after being severely tipped to favor one side. How did it happen? What lessons can you draw from that experience that you could use in your own relations with people from other groups?

51   PRACTICE CO-CREATIVITY

One of the ways to experience equal power is to be creative together in solving shared problems. Co-creativity has two elements: *co,* meaning together, with each other; and *creativity,* meaning the ability to generate new ideas and possibilities for action.

The "together" part requires that we make contact with people who are different from us and establish ways for working together. The "creativity" part requires that we activate that part of our brains that is able to be imaginative, intuitive, and full of wonder and awe.

- Find or create a situation where you can work with people from another group on issues that concern you both. It may be issues about your relationship, or it may be other issues that both groups have some interest in.

· Before you address the problem or issue you are concerned with, take some time to warm up your creative juices.

· Together, learn and practice the process of brainstorming, where as a group you throw out as many ideas as possible on a particular subject, without judging or discussing anything until a large list has been made. People are invited to piggy-back on each other's ideas, to make silly and outrageous suggestions, and to aim for quantity, not quality.

· Try other creative exercises. Practice the "rule of seven," where for every problem each person must come up with seven suggestions. Compare your lists to see how many good ideas came from the group as a whole. Or, practice seeing a familiar object in an unfamiliar way. For instance, turn a chair over and name, together, all the things it could be.

· Now that your creative juices are flowing, apply that openness to a real problem, working together as a group to find creative solutions to familiar difficulties.

52   ENGAGE IN HONEST CONVERSATION

Even with all our goodwill for co-existence and the honoring of diversity, there can be real obstacles to good intergroup relations. Many of them come from painful history that has never been healed or resolved. Others come from continuing structures and norms in society that make it difficult to sustain equality and fairness.

Even if we can't cure all the ills and resolve all the distrust and animosity that may have built up over time, we can at least begin by being honest with each other about what the obstacles are. This is a good place to start.

· Convene or participate in intergroup dialogues (interfaith, interracial, inter-ethnic, intergenerational). Bring in a facilitator to help the group if the topics are too hot to handle on your own. Commit to an ongoing process.

· Be willing to have an honest conversation. Let yourselves look at the hard places as they truly are. No need to run away, make it seem better than it is, or pretend there is an easy fix. Just be fully present to the truth of each side's experience.

• Acknowledge the need for healing and reconciliation where there has been pain and suffering. (The next chapter will go into more detail about how to do this.)

• Develop confidence-building measures. Find small things that each side can do, separately or together, to increase trust and improve confidence. Move beyond words to practical actions. See if, and how, this changes the conversation.

53   HELP THEM TO HELP YOU

In our search for co-existence, we often have unrealistic expectations that the other group will meet our needs once we tell them where we stand. It doesn't work that way. They are busy putting forward their needs and positions and expecting us to satisfy them.

To make progress in being a peace-able community, we have to help others help us to get our interests met. We have to make it easy and attractive for them to meet us halfway. We have to find a way to assure them that by being more friendly with us, they are not losing but gaining.

• Be inviting. In informal interactions and more formal dialogues, forgo the urge to be critical and negative. Instead, keep the door open to harmonious relations. Let others know that you're interested in moving forward, in improving the relationship.

• Go step by step. Don't try to do too much at one time. Relationships that have been difficult for some time will take time to change. Take simple action steps that have a high likelihood of success. In that way, confidence builds.

• Help everyone save face. Saving "face" means being able to feel respected, to walk with dignity. To change, to compromise a long-standing position, to make a new start, we must be able to move forward without humiliation, shame, or guilt. Offer suggestions that are easy for others to say "Yes" to; suggestions where everyone can feel and look good.

• Give and seek information. Ask, "What would it take to move this relationship to a better place?" Share the same information from your point of view. Take as much time as you need to gather as much information as necessary, so you can address the real issues successfully.

54 PLAY TOGETHER

One of the best ways to break the distrust and hostility that can build between groups is to move away from the hard issues into a social mode. While we might not agree on ideological issues, or on the painful parts of our history, we can enjoy a meal together.

Play is a way of connecting with the core of our shared human experience. Laughter, fun, relaxation, and joy can bring people together in the heart, where our oneness transcends our differences. We all want to be happy. Finding ways to be happy together can build strong bridges over even the deepest canyons.

• Organize picnics. A picnic is a great way to be together informally. In many cultures, sharing food is an act of friendship. Being outdoors, where people can play games and move around, promotes a sense of ease and possibility.

• Do sports activities together. More formal than a picnic, sports provide a direct avenue for relating. If the chosen sport is a team sport, used mixed teams as a way of diffusing the intergroup rivalries and demonstrating that the groups can indeed work together.

• Celebrate each other's holidays. Invite people from another group to join you in a holiday special to your people. By sharing our culture—with all the rituals, music, food, and drink that are often part of holiday cheer—we help break down stereotypes and build a sense of familiarity.

• Bring the children together. Nothing builds a sense of community faster than seeing children together. Children do not naturally carry the fears, prejudices, or historical wounds of our intergroup relations (unless we adults have taught them to), so they are happy to play and laugh and make new friends. That can pave the way for the parents to make new friends too.

REVIEW

Practice the Four Principles of Peace and Co-Existence

COMMUNITY
Celebrate our differences in order to honor our unity.

COOPERATION
Use co-creativity to address
intergroup difficulties more effectively.

NONVIOLENCE
Engage in honest conversation about the
obstacles in the relationship, and build trust.

WITNESS
Honor the humanity of all through play and laughter.

CONFRONTING RACISM, TOGETHER

*Racism is a particularly deep and ongoing wound in U.S. society.
It is difficult for well-meaning white people, especially, to acknowledge their collusion with racism. This story tells about a courageous
moment in an interfaith, interracial dialogue when blacks and
whites together could break the ice of formality and begin a meaningful and honest conversation.*

That the congregation at my synagogue was all white goes without
saying. When our new rabbi suggested an interfaith dialogue with an
all-black church from another part of town, we welcomed the opportunity to expand our horizons.

The meetings went well at first, but were, frankly, rather bland. No
one wanted to say anything to offend the others. Everyone outdid themselves showing hospitality and courtesy. We certainly didn't think we
were racist in any way, and wanted to make sure our new friends understood that.

The first crack in the foundation appeared when we made our first
visit to their church. We were invited to sit in on a Bible study class one
evening. Quietly, among ourselves, we wondered if it was safe to go to
that neighborhood at night, and we made sure we traveled in groups.
Then we felt guilty about being scared—did that mean we were racist?

At the next meeting, one man from the church asked a difficult
question: What was your first experience with an African American
person? I remembered Betty, the maid who worked for us when I was a
child. Soon it became evident that many of us in the congregation met
the black community first through our maids. When the second, then
the third person admitted that, it got very awkward. With the fourth
person, the tension rose to an almost unbearable level. By the time the
fifth person said, "Me too," somehow that broke down the wall, and
there was nothing to do but laugh that ironic laugh that says, "Oh yeah,
that's how it is." In that moment we saw laid bare before us the perva-
sive poison of racism, and how we were all damaged by it in different
ways. That was the moment the long journey of healing could begin.

RESOURCE GUIDE

Check within your local community for opportunities for inter-racial or interfaith dialogue, antiracism activities, and multicultural events. Here are some suggestions:

PROGRAMS AND ORGANIZATIONS

HOPE IN THE CITIES

Working to build communities of hope, security, and opportunity by exploring new frontiers in race relations. Partner cities are matched throughout the United States and around the world.
RICHMOND, VA; PHONE: 804-358-1764; FAX: 804-358-1769;
E-MAIL: hopecities@aol.com;
WEB SITE: www.hopeinthecities.org

NATIONAL ASSOCIATION FOR MULTICULTURAL EDUCATION

A membership organization for teachers and administrators from early childhood through higher education, and others interested in addressing issues of diversity, multicultural education, educational equity, and social justice.
WASHINGTON, DC; PHONE: 202-628-6263; FAX: 202-628-6264;
E-MAIL: name@nameorg.org;
WEB SITE: www.nameorg.org

NATIONAL COALITION BUILDING INSTITUTE

Works to eliminate prejudice and intergroup conflict in communi-ties around the world. Trains local leadership teams in schools, cor-porations, prisons, governments, and other settings. Offers tools for working through tough, polarizing intergroup issues.
WASHINGTON, DC; PHONE: 202-785-9400; FAX: 202-785-3385;
E-MAIL: ncbiinc@aol.com; WEB SITE: www.ncbi.org

THE NATIONAL MULTICULTURAL INSTITUTE

Seeks to increase communication, understanding, and respect among people of different racial, ethnic, and cultural backgrounds, and to provide a forum for discussion of the critical issues of multiculturalism facing our society. Resources, conferences, and training.
WASHINGTON, DC; PHONE: 202-483-0700, FAX: 202-483-5233; E-MAIL: nmci@nmci.org; WEB SITE: www.nmci.org

THE COEXISTENCE INITIATIVE

Seeks to catalyze a global awareness of, and commitment to, creating a world safe for differences. Offers a newsletter, web site, resource center, workshops, and special projects.
NEW YORK, NY; PHONE: 212-303-9445, FAX: 212-980-4027; E-MAIL: info@coexistence.net; WEB SITE: www.coexistence.net

BOOKS, TAPES, VIDEOS

Afraid of the Dark: What Whites and Blacks Need to Know About Each Other. Jim Myers. Lawrence Hill & Co., 2000.

A Peacock in the Land of Penguins: A Tale of Diversity and Discovery. Barbara Hateley, et al. Berrett-Koehler, 1997.

A Public Peace Process: Sustained Dialogue to Transform Racial and Ethnic Conflicts. Harold Saunders, St. Martin's Press, 1999.

WEB SITES

ANTIRACISMNET

Articles, resources, discussions, action alerts, and news about antiracism.
www.igc.org/igc/gateway/arnindex.html

Keywords to explore through your computer search engine: *race relations, racism, diversity, interfaith dialogue*

SEVEN

PEACE & RECONCILIATION
Healing Our Broken Heart

We are broken,
And we will not be mended
Until we remember
That we are unbreakable.
—LOUISE DIAMOND

Conflict hurts—physically, mentally, emotionally, and spiritually. In our personal and group relationships, we may know loss, abandonment, abuse, betrayal, or rejection.

This hurt, if left untended, can fester. It can leave a legacy of anguish. Our hearts close up; they become hardened against those who have hurt us. We become defensive or aggressive.

Peace requires healing and reconciliation. What appears broken must and can be mended, if we are to know peace as a way of life. We must re-establish the bonds that have been broken through discord, and learn to live again in open-hearted love.

Sometimes the people we need to reconcile with are not physically available, or they don't want to do the healing work with us. Sometimes our grievances are against a whole group, or "the system," making it hard to find a partner in the healing process. That's okay. We do what we can by ourselves, or with whomever is willing to join us in this healing journey. We start; we do the best we can, one step at a time, regardless of what the other party does or doesn't do.

55   KNOW THAT YOU ARE UNBREAKABLE

In one way, you can be hurt. In another way, nothing can hurt you. How is this possible?

This is so because human beings have a deep inner essence that is naturally whole and perfect. No matter what happens in the day-to-day drama of our lives, within the center core of our being is that vast pool of soulforce that we have called our "natural self." At the level of the natural self, peace and wholeness simply are. The words themselves, *whole, holy,* and *heal,* mean the same thing. To heal is to remember who you really are—a child of the universe, divine and loving and inherently whole.

• Remember your natural self. Go back to the first chapter of this book and recall how to find your place of inner peace. Confirm and affirm that at your center, which is open like the sky, nothing can hurt you.

• Trace a pathway to this place so you can go there whenever you want. Use an image, a word, or a gesture to be a signpost for your journey home, to remind you of the way when you feel lost.

• Test your unbreakability. Think of a situation where your heart has been hurt. Now center home. Feel the hurt wash over you, like a wave passing over a rock. And like a wave, it rises and falls away. Your center remains strong and clear.

56   SPEAK THE TRUTH OF YOUR EXPERIENCE

To start the healing journey, you need to express what happened to you that was hurtful. Although other people will have a different version of what happened, you need to touch and tell the truth of your own experience. That is your truth; no one can judge or dismiss your feelings.

Sharing your experience out loud (or in writing, drawing, or movement) is the way to begin to clear the debris that has piled up in your heart. It starts things moving, opening channels and doorways for love to grow again.

- Tell your story. Your story is important. It is how you make sense out of what happened to you, how you understand the context and experience of your pain. Being able to say it, to present it as a narrative, allows you to give meaning to your world, and allows those who listen to understand how you feel.

- Tell your story again. Repeating the story—to yourself, to others—gives you the chance to start to disidentify from it. The story is your experience, but it isn't you. In fact, as you tell the story again and again, the emotional charge in it may begin to dissolve, and you can get a more objective perspective on what happened.

- Tell your story a different way. Adopt some other point of view or a different emphasis. This may give you and your listener new understanding and information about the experience. It may provide a whole other slant on things.

57   ACKNOWLEDGE THE HURT

We all want the hurt that we feel to be acknowledged. We want someone to notice, to care. We especially want those who have hurt us to realize what they have done and take responsibility for it.

We cannot demand this from others, but we can give it. Every damaged relationship has two sides to it. Each party, regardless of who started the conflict, has contributed something to the harm.

- Listen to the other party's story with the same respect you wish for yours. Everyone in the conflict has the truth of their experience, as you have yours. Indeed, there are many truths existing at the same time.

- Listen carefully to hear how the other's story makes sense to them. If you begin to feel defensive or argumentative, just breathe and let it go, so you can be fully present to their pain.

• Acknowledge the suffering of the one who is sharing with you. Just let them know that you hear how they hurt. Affirm their feelings, which is separate from judging who did what to whom and why. The hurt is real, however it happened.

• Look honestly at how your own thoughts or actions may have contributed to the other party's suffering. Even if you think your behavior was justified by what they did to you first, still, own up to your own contribution in keeping the conflict going. Take responsibility for your actions.

58   APOLOGIZE

Saying "I'm sorry" can seem like a difficult thing to do. We can think up all kinds of reasons why "It wasn't my fault." We (or our group) did something harmful because . . . we were only protecting ourselves or our legitimate rights; we were only responding to what was done to us; we didn't realize it would make so much trouble. There are plenty of excuses and justifications for our actions.

Having the courage for peace means being willing to say "Sorry." Only by apology can we begin to mend a broken trust. Only with a true sense of remorse and request for forgiveness can we start healing the wounded hearts.

• Do you feel true remorse? Let yourself sink in to the knowledge that you (or your group) caused pain to another. Can you feel sadness for that? If you cannot feel truly contrite—sorry for the pain you've caused—then you are probably still defending yourself to yourself. Can you stop that long enough to feel regret for your part in the situation?

• Express your regrets. Once you feel genuinely contrite, express your regrets to the person or people you have offended. A simple "I'm sorry," or "Please forgive me," can go a long way toward reconciliation.

• Be specific. Say what you are sorry about. Let it come from your heart. Let your sadness and regret show. Say what you did, and let the other person know that you see how it hurt them. They may not respond in kind. It doesn't matter. You can only take responsibility for yourself.

59 FORGIVE

The other side of apology is forgiveness. Forgiveness is something that happens first in your own heart. You cannot force it. When you're ready and willing to let go of your anger and desire for blame and revenge, then you can release yourself from that burden. You surrender that pain, freeing yourself of its weight.

Forgiveness does not mean you forget, excuse, or condone what was done to you. You can still find the action unacceptable, but you forgive the person for doing it.

When your heart has forgiven, you may choose to extend that to the one who hurt you. By letting them know you have forgiven them (whether they have apologized or not), you make room for a new opening in the relationship.

• Notice what negative feelings you are carrying about what some person (or group) did that hurt you. Notice how carrying those feelings affects your body, your mind, your heart.

• Test if you are ready to surrender, or let go of, those feelings. Imagine being free of them. Can you do it, or do you want to hang on to them? If so, why?

• When you are ready, find a way to release what you are holding. Give it to God, to the Earth, to the wind or water; give it up or put it down, or whatever language works for you. Just let it go. Breathe deeply. Feel the new space opening in your heart.

• If appropriate, share with the person who hurt you that you forgive them.

• You may want to create some ritual of forgiveness, either alone or with the other(s) involved. A simple ritual can give deep and lasting meaning to the act of forgiveness. The ritual can be anything you want—it can include anything from nature, a candle, a formal sharing of words, a feast—whatever lends significance to the event for you.

• Above all, forgive yourself. Whatever you've done in the situation—even the negative feelings you've held about the other that have blocked the healing—you can also let go of. Forgiving yourself brings you back to center, and to a fresh start with your own heart.

60   RIGHT THE WRONGS

Saying "Sorry" is not the end of reconciliation. Remedial action may also be necessary. If we make a mess, we need to clean it up. What can you do to make amends, to fix what is broken? This helps bring closure, and a sense of justice, to the situation.

· Stop the hurting behavior. Once we have acknowledged the pain we have caused, felt remorse, and offered an apology, we cannot continue the same behavior that caused the hurt. We must stop doing it and make a clear commitment not to do it again.

· Fix the damage. If you have destroyed something physical, replace it. If you have harmed something emotional, find out what you can do to heal it. Find out what would make it better, and negotiate a reasonable, do-able plan to repair the damage.

· Make symbolic amends. Sometimes it is not possible to fix the actual harm. In that case, a symbolic offering can serve a similar purpose. Many cultures use restitution or compensation to restore harmony. Find a meaningful gesture that is agreed to by both parties.

· Work for institutional changes. When the reconciliation is at a group level, the damage is usually perpetuated by unjust institutional structures. For instance, healing the damage from the slave trade requires looking at ongoing racial discrimination in our society. Commit to righting the historical wrongs at the societal level.

· Ask for what you want. If you are the one on the receiving end of an apology, say what you need to bring the relationship back to harmony. Tell the one who hurt you what they can do to make amends; help them find a way to complete the reconciliation process.

61   MOURN FULLY

When we lose something important to us—something tangible, like someone we love or our home, or something intangible, like a sense of safety or trust—we are sad. When someone else has taken what we care about away from us, we are doubly sad.

Loss is like a stone in the heart. We need to grieve and mourn our loss, to wash that stone away with our tears. If we don't complete this process, the stone will stay in our heart and weigh us down.

• Recognize the loss. Sometimes, in our painful situations with others, we don't even realize that we have lost something of value. The circumstances may seem like a fight, or a rejection, or an injustice. Beneath that, however, there is likely to be some part of our dreams, our dignity, our sense of worth, or our sense of safety in the world that is lost.

• Let yourself feel the range of feelings. When we suffer loss, we are sad, but we are also likely to be angry. We may also be afraid that what we suffered will happen again, or that we'll never recover. Trust that this whole range of feelings is natural, and may come and go in cycles over time.

• Express your feelings. Crying is a good release, one that we may need to repeat again and again when our loss is big. Find creative ways to express anger and fear without hurting yourself or another. Keep your emotions moving; otherwise they get stuck and you cannot heal.

• Ask for spiritual and emotional help. In some situations, the loss is just too big to handle alone. Calling for help from God, or whatever your sense of a higher power might be, can bring great comfort. You might also seek counseling—pastoral or otherwise. Many big cities have grief centers or special programs for people struggling to heal from abuse, violence, or other trauma.

• Do some grieving ritual to bring closure. When the grief has run its course, or to help it on the way, it is useful to do some ritual to acknowledge an ending and a new beginning. Design your own ritual to bring a sense of completion to the mourning process.

62   LOOK AT HISTORICAL PATTERNS

Sometimes the pain in our relationships feels eerily familiar. We may feel that we been here before. That's because we tend to repeat patterns of relationship until we figure out the pattern and how to change it.

In our group relations, deep-rooted conflicts will occur in cycles. There may be periods of quiet in between periods of violence. We may inherit stories and myths about the conflict from our parents or grandparents, and feel we are still fighting the same fight. The Four Principles of Peace can help us break these cycles.

· Think of a relationship that is distressing you. Does the situation feel familiar? What does it remind you of? Have you experienced something like this before? How is this the same, and how is it different?

· Can you identify the pattern that is repeating itself? Give it a name. (For instance, this is the Betrayal scenario, or a case of Blame the Victim.) What is the basic story line of the pattern? This gives you some perspective on the pattern.

· If the pattern has a story line, how could you change the story to change the pattern? What can you personally do to make it different? What could other people do? Since we can't control other people's behavior, focus on your own power to try new behavior.

· Do the unexpected. If the story line suggests a certain course of action, do something entirely different and unusual. See what effect that might have on changing the dynamics.

· If the pattern is a hand-me-down from earlier generations, make a commitment not to pass it along to the next generation. Do whatever it takes to break the cycle.

63   LET LOVE FLOW

Peace is love in action. When we have been hurt in our relationships, we close our hearts. Like Pharaoh in Egypt, we harden our hearts against those whom we perceive as harming us. Until our hardened hearts can be softened, and love—which is our natural state—can flow freely, we cannot be in peace.

Love is like a river. It flows until it comes to some obstacle that blocks the way. Then the water backs up or gets diverted. The need for reconciliation is like a dam in the stream of our loving nature. We must remove the dam so the river of our lifeforce, our love force, can move on to the great ocean.

• Imagine your heart melting. Think of a situation where you have hardened your heart toward someone or some group. Picture how your heart is tight, closed, hard. Now imagine it melting, softening, opening. What do you notice?

• Think of someone you love deeply, with whom there are no obstacles. Feel your open-hearted, unconditional, boundless love for that person. Now think of someone (or group) with whom you are in conflict or by whom you feel hurt. How does your heart feel now? Experiment with feeling that first sense of pure love toward your "opponent." Can you do it, even for a brief moment?

• Find something to appreciate about your "opponent." They can't be all bad. What's one quality that you like about them, one thing that they've done that you truly respect?

• Be grateful. Some say that our greatest enemy is our greatest teacher, for he gives us the opportunity to learn and grow in patience and compassion and teaches us about reconciliation and love. Think of your "opponent" with gratitude for all the lessons you can learn through this relationship.

REVIEW

Practice the Four Principles of Peace and Reconciliation

COMMUNITY
Realize that you and your "opponent" are in this together.
Saying "Sorry" and making amends can help keep the heart open.

COOPERATION
Work with your "opponent" to create meaningful healing rituals.

NONVIOLENCE
Stop hurting and start healing. Take the
first step by forgiving yourself and others.

WITNESS
Remember that you are unbreakable,
and that your true nature is love.

OPENING THE HEART WITH "SORRY"

Sometimes we don't even know we have something to apologize for. We may be fighting about this or that, but until we touch the place of deepest hurt, we cannot start the healing process. It helps when our friends tell us how we have hurt them, so we can acknowledge what we have done and ask forgiveness. In this story, a woman realizes, for the first time, how much she has hurt her husband, and offers a heartfelt apology.

In a divorce mediation session, my two clients were struggling hard over every issue they had to deal with. Finally, I asked to see each of them privately. The wife said to me that she felt annoyed at her husband's inability to be clear and to know what he wanted. Privately, the husband said that he was having a hard time, as he always did, talking with her. I asked him to explore this more, which he did. I then asked what of this he wanted to share with his wife.

Back in joint session the husband said, "I always am aware of how smart you are and what a good mother you are. I start feeling like I can't ever be what you are so I get unsure and awkward. I know I annoy you—I can see your irritation. Then I get more unsure."

The wife thought for a moment and said, "I am sorry that I have contributed to that feeling for you—that should not happen." After a moment's silence, there was the sound of soft crying. The husband said, "Thank you. Did you know that in 17 years of marriage you never apologized once to me?"

The wife looked startled, and then blurted out, "You are right, I could never allow myself to feel like I was wrong. I'm so sorry."

From this honest moment, the couple was able to move ahead with a new level of genuine appreciation for one another.

RESOURCE GUIDE

Check within your local community for restorative justice programs, reconciliation dialogues, and grief centers. Here are some suggestions:

PROGRAMS AND ORGANIZATIONS

INITIATIVES OF CHANGE

An international network of people working for reconciliation, justice, and the healing of history. Its Agenda for Reconciliation program works globally to foster peace through acknowledgement of past wrongs, apology, restitution, and forgiveness.

WASHINGTON, DC; PHONE: 202-872-9077; FAX: 202-872-9137;
E-MAIL: info@initiativesofchange.org;
WEB SITE: www.us.initiativesofchange.org

ONE BY ONE

A nonprofit organization created by Jews and Christians whose lives have been deeply affected by the Holocaust. Holds dialogues among descendants of survivors, perpetrators, bystanders, and resisters, allowing compassionate listening to one another's stories of pain, guilt, anguish, loss, and fear.

BROOKLINE, MA; PHONE: 617-424-1540; FAX: 413-256-1804;
E-MAIL: droth@crocker.com; WEB SITE: www-one-by-one.org

VICTIM OFFENDER RECONCILIATION PROGRAM

Seeks to bring restorative justice reform to our criminal and juvenile justice systems and to empower victims, offenders, and communities to heal the effects of crime. Offers articles, training, conferences and public education, technical assistance, consulting, and victim-offender mediation and reconciliation services.

CAMAS, WA; PHONE: 360-260-1551; FAX: 360-260-1563;
E-MAIL: martyprice@vorp.com; WEB SITE: www.vorp.com

BOOKS, TAPES, VIDEOS

Forgiveness: Breaking the Chain of Hate. Michael Henderson. Bookpartners, 1999.

Healing Anger. His Holiness the Dalai Lama. Snow Lion Publications, 1997.

The Journey Toward Reconciliation. John Paul Lederach. Herald Press, 1999.

No Future Without Forgiveness. Desmond Tutu. Doubleday & Co., 2000.

WEB SITES

CLOSE THE BOOK ON HATE

A joint national campaign of the Anti-Defamation League (ADL) and Barnes & Noble, Inc., to provide children and their parents, caregivers, teachers, and civic leaders with the tools, resources, and programs to better understand and help eliminate prejudice and discrimination in their communities.
www.adl.org/ctboh

Keywords to explore through your computer search engine: *reconciliation, forgiveness, healing, compassion*

EIGHT

PEACE & SOCIAL CHANGE
... With Justice for All

*The only thing necessary for the triumph of evil
is for good men (and women) to do nothing.*
—EDMUND BURKE

Our society, having not yet adopted the Four Principles of Peace, promotes social, political, and economic conditions that allow some to thrive at the expense of others. This may show up as relatively invisible norms that stack the deck against people of a certain race, class, gender, sexual orientation, age, or other category of our rich diversity. Or it may take the form of outright exploitation or oppression of many for the benefit of a few.

If we want real peace in our lives and in the world, we cannot go along with injustice. We must work for social change, both at the level of root causes and also on a case-by-case basis. Some of us are activists, taking to the streets to protest and call attention to the wrongs we wish to right. Others of us act quietly, through letter writing, involvement in local projects, and individual action. What is important is that people stand up and say "No!" to the injustices, for they flourish only to the extent we allow them to.

In addition to protesting against the wrongs, we must also work to build new forms and institutions that support the rights of all people to live with freedom, equality, and dignity. This is where we have the chance to be warriors for peace.

64 INFORM YOURSELF

There are many causes to choose from in our work for social change: poverty, human rights abuses, hunger, racism, sexism, and all the other "isms" that discriminate on the basis of identity; the proliferation of nuclear and conventional weapons; sweat-shop economics—the list is long. We can choose to work locally, in our own communities and nation, or for causes around the world.

Our tendency is to see "black and white," "good guys and bad guys" on these kinds of hot topics; the reality is much more complex. That is why we need to inform ourselves from many perspectives.

• Determine what issue calls you to action—where are you drawn to make a difference, to help alleviate suffering?

• Get curious. Ask questions to understand root causes; find out what approaches seem to be most effective in addressing these problems.

• Browse the Internet. Type your keyword into a search engine and scroll through the many items that appear, reading the ones that catch your attention.

• Go to the library or the bookstore for books, newspapers, and magazine articles on your subject.

• Talk with volunteers, professionals, academic experts. Above all, talk directly with those who endure the hardships associated with this issue. Talk also with those on the other side, to understand their point of view and to search for common ground.

• Find organizations in your community that address these concerns—your place of worship is a good place to start. Explore what they are doing, and how you might get involved.

• As you educate yourself, listen for how you can make your unique contribution. Listen for your way to become a warrior for peace.

65   BECOME A HUMAN RIGHTS ADVOCATE

To be a human being means to be endowed, as the U.S. Declaration of Independence says, with certain "inalienable rights." Freedom of speech, of religious expression, of association; freedom from slavery, tyranny, oppression—these and many others are our human birthright.

We are entitled to be treated with dignity and respect, regardless of our color, gender, nationality, age. Every day and in every country human rights are ignored or violated, on purpose or as a by-product of some other action. Peace requires vigilance and action to insure the rights of all, for anyone—individual or group—who is denied their basic rights cannot take their true place in the family of life.

To be an advocate for human rights means to work for the rights of others. It means to speak out, to witness, to watch, and to act so that no one may abuse another with impunity.

• Read the UN Universal Declaration of Human Rights. Discuss it with family and friends, with coworkers, at your place of worship.

• Pick a topic of human rights that particularly interests you—for example, child labor, sex slavery, torture, prisoners of conscience, the death penalty, sweat shops, ethnic cleansing, racial discrimination. Educate yourself on the subject. Find organizations working on that issue, and join them or support their work.

• Follow human rights news. Pick a place where human rights is an ongoing concern and subscribe to an Internet news service that reports on that subject regularly.

• Understand also the universal responsibilities that balance our universal rights—the responsibility to honor life, to respect differences, to be accountable for our actions, to use shared resources appropriately. Take care to articulate these responsibilities, and live them fully in your daily life. Teach them to your children. See that they are taught in your school system.

• Be vigilant with your own political leaders, bosses at work, religious leaders, and others who hold power over the lives and fates of many, to ensure they act always with the greatest integrity.

66 EXERCISE YOUR OPPORTUNITIES FOR DEMOCRACY

Change—peaceful, democratic change—is possible. Although there are entrenched interests that may seem to have a tight grip on maintaining the status quo for their own benefit, still we know that if people speak and act effectively, things can change.

Many of us who live in democratic countries, especially the United States, take democracy for granted. We complain about all the things that are wrong, but we neglect to take the actions open to us to fix them. Yet in a flourishing democracy, we have three essential tools for social change: speaking out, acting together, and choosing our leaders.

• Pick one issue of public policy that interests you passionately. Educate yourself about it.

• Go to public forums where this issue is being discussed or decided. Speak your mind. Listen to other views respectfully. Try to build consensus around points of common ground.

• Write letters to the editor or articles for publication; go on the radio or public access television to get your views across. Invite responses, open the door for dialogue.

• Find organizations working on this issue, and join their efforts.

• Question candidates for public office about their stand on your issue. Educate them; lobby them. If you don't find someone you like, consider running for office yourself, or find someone who would represent your views.

• Vote! Make your voice heard in every election, no matter how small the office.

67   TAKE A PERSONAL PRIVILEGE INVENTORY

Many of us live in a state of greater privilege than someone else, or some other group. We may have more money, connections, or status due to a variety of factors (race, gender, class, religion, education level) that make it easier for us to succeed in the world than for others who lack our resources. Privilege usually translates into power.

We do not need to feel guilty about our privilege. We do need, however, to acknowledge and understand it. Then we can use it as a gift, to serve others, in the search for social justice.

1   Take the following self-inventory, to understand your own relative privilege—and lack thereof. On the chart following, for each item in the horizontal line, place a dot on the upward scale to indicate where you have greater privilege than others (1 being the least; 5 being the most).

2   Place a dot on the downward scale to show where you have less privilege than others (again, 1 being the least and 5 being the most). On any one item, you may have both greater and lesser privilege than others, depending on what category of others you are considering.

3   Now connect the dots. This will give you a graphic view of your state of personal privilege. Examine this graph to see what information emerges for you.

4   Take some action on that information, to use your special privilege to help others.

PERSONAL PRIVILEGE INVENTORY

5
4
3
2
1
Race Class Gender Wealth Education Ethnicity Work Religion Other (specify) (x)
1
2
3
4
5
(y)

68   EMPOWER THE POWERLESS

From your Personal Privilege Inventory you may have found areas where you have more access and power in society than others. There are other people, by virtue of the various factors noted, that have less power in society. Think how you can help them become more powerful.

Empowering others means providing opportunities; it does not mean giving something away or doing something for someone that they can do for themselves. Empowering others means helping them work for their own goals, not imposing your goals on them. It means opening doors, encouraging, supporting others on their journey toward dignity and equality.

· Be a tutor to help teach a young child with learning disabilities how to read; a refugee how to pass the citizenship test; a school dropout how to practice a trade.

· Make a job available for someone who might otherwise have difficulty finding work; select an often passed-over candidate for a promotion; encourage job-training programs at your workplace.

· Support an ethnic or racial group in its struggle for justice and the opportunity to participate fully in society as first class citizens.

· Volunteer your time at a legal aid project, a battered woman's shelter, a free medical clinic, an adult literacy program, an indigenous rights organization, a mental health facility, a homeless shelter.

· Give to a scholarship fund for Third World students, striving artists, the rural poor, or any other group of students often overlooked in the scholarship process.

· Coach sports at a youth center; support the Special Olympics, or advocate for recreational sports programs for the physically challenged.

69   BE A VOICE FOR THE VOICELESS

Some people and groups in society are so powerless that they have no real voice. Their needs get drowned out by the majority or dominant group in the culture. They are not represented in places of power, so their concerns are not considered. They are marginalized in the economic, social, and political fabric of society and may need someone to speak for them in places where they cannot speak for themselves.

Others, by virtue of their identity group, are looked down upon by those in power. They are the butt of jokes and belittling comments. They are referred to in demeaning or patronizing terms. They too need someone to speak on their behalf, especially when they are not present to do so for themselves.

Giving voice to the voiceless means standing up for their rights in settings where you have more power and presence than they. It means confronting inappropriate behavior and insisting on respectful treatment for those who are considered "less than," "not like us," or "not good enough."

• Do not allow prejudicial, stereotypical, or belittling speech about others to pass unchallenged. Confront all instances of "hate speech," whether subtle or overt. Refuse to allow slurs to be made about others, even in jest.

• Represent the interests of the voiceless in settings where they are either not present or not allowed a full voice. Do this even if you do not necessarily agree with their position.

• Make the invisible visible in any setting where decisions are being made that will affect them. Bring the uninvited to the party, the voiceless into the conversation. You can do this by actually including people from the disempowered groups in settings where important things are happening, or by speaking on their behalf.

70   PRACTICE MORAL WITNESS AND SOLIDARITY

Ultimately, social justice is about morality. What is right and wrong in how we treat each other? To act for social change is to be a witness for what is morally and ethically correct in our human relationships.

To witness for something means to stand up and be counted. We may practice silent witness—holding a silent, candlelit vigil in honor of some oppressed individual or group—or we may practice active witness though showing up and speaking up for the marginalized and vulnerable among us. The power of witness is tremendous. It has a great effect in getting people's attention and changing hearts, including our own as the one who witnesses. To witness is to say, "I am here; I will not be moved; I see; I take notice; I hold you accountable."

Solidarity means that we recognize our oneness with the oppressed. What happens to them happens to us. We stand with them to give support, to let them know they are not alone, to share and thereby ease the burden of their suffering.

• Again, pick the issue of your choice, the individuals or group you wish to stand with. Find a way to be physically present to them in a time of need. Let your presence speak your values.

• Align yourself with the experience of the ones you have chosen to witness for. Live as they live, suffer with them; leave your privilege at the door for a while, and put yourself in their shoes.

• Ask yourself the hard questions. How far you will go to protect the rights of those you are in solidarity with? Will you put your body on the line for them? Your freedom? Your life? There are no right or wrong answers; what's important is to know where you stand and what your limits are.

• Be attentive that your advocacy on behalf of others does not cast the perpetrators as inhuman demons, thereby increasing hostility and "us versus them" thinking. Think of the perpetrators of injustice with compassion; you can feel compassion for the person without condoning the behavior. Even those guilty of committing the worst evil acts are human beings in need of compassion. Their suffering is also great, because they have become so disconnected from their true and natural selves.

71 WORK FROM THE
BOTTOM UP AND THE TOP DOWN

Social change, to be lasting, must occur through the whole fabric of society. The motivation for change comes from two directions: either there is a compelling vision of where we want to go, or there is so much hurt that we want it to stop—or both. Since the ones on "top" in any society rarely feel the pain, in a sincere way, of those without power, that motivation will usually come from the grassroots, or bottom up.

The bottom up approach to social justice is strong; it is democracy at its best. It involves people in shaping their own destiny; it empowers people to work together for common cause; it informs and engages people in acts of shared meaning; it builds community; it airs the underside of public life, bringing into the light that which needs to be changed. It also can be very effective.

Change from the bottom up is even more effective when met by change from the top down. For true transformation, this meeting point is necessary. While the momentum for social change will usually come from the grassroots, still, in every powerful institution there are individuals who do have a vision for a better way and who do feel the hurt of the people. As they become more visible and credible, much is possible.

• Find your grassroots allies for community action. Help articulate a compelling vision for a better future, and express the pain of the current situation in ways that can be truly heard and understood.

• Seek out those in the top levels of political, economic, and social institutions who share that vision. Make common cause with them. Help them to help you by avoiding blame, finger pointing, and the casting of those at the top as the enemy. Consider how you can work together.

• Explore the meeting point of the top down and bottom up approaches. Who is in the middle? What institutions can influence both the people and those who hold the power? How can you best work with and through them?

• Realize that there is great power—and powerlessness—in each position of the system: top, bottom, and middle. Seek to change situations of "power over" to ones of "power with," so that everyone can share in the benefits of change.

72 WORK WITH OTHERS FOR STRUCTURAL CHANGE

Lasting social change needs to happen at three levels: the political (decision-making arena); the social (the hearts and minds of the people); and the structural (the institutions that define the structure of society). The structural level is the hardest to change because there is great inertia and a strong habit of beliefs and behaviors that support the status quo.

We know that inertia can be overcome when there is enough momentum. Momentum comes from joining forces, building movements and cooperative alliances. We also know that large-scale action, to be effective, must be well organized and free from the infighting and power struggles that sap such efforts.

• Find your social change partners. Join with organizations that are doing the kind of work you support.

• Be daring in your choice of allies. Build revolutionary partnerships—look for individuals and groups that you might never have thought of as logical partners, perhaps those who occupy a position far from yours on the spectrum. Sometimes the most effective links are the ones that seem the least likely, where people have to come from great distances to find their common interests.

• Build alliances, coalitions, and movements. Joined forces are more powerful than individual ones.

• Seek out the institutions that can most effect change—those that shape the lives of many, such as the media, the educational process, religion, business associations, political parties. Work within these systems for the structural changes that will replace a culture of discrimination, abuse of power, and lack of respect with one that is empowering and inclusive of all.

• Be patient yet persistent. Social change—building a culture of peace—takes time and sustained effort. Support one another in remaining hopeful and in trusting the ultimate success of your mission.

REVIEW

Practice the Four Principles of Peace and Social Change

COMMUNITY
Honor the dignity of all, and work for social justice.

COOPERATION
Find allies and partners in the search for structural change.

NONVIOLENCE
Keep the dialogue going, especially
with those you see as oppressors.

WITNESS
Be a living witness for peace.

GETTING INVOLVED

A lot of people notice the injustices of our society but never seem to find the time or energy to do something concrete about them. The man in this story was like that for a long time, until one day he got motivated to action. By involving his friends and colleagues, he was able to catalyze meaningful change in his community.

Some people turn away when they see the homeless on the streets, with their shopping carts and cardboard tents. Not me—I always stop on my way to work and say, "Hello, how're you doing?" and offer spare change. I've come close to losing my own home through financial difficulties, so I understand how vulnerable we all can be.

I never thought of myself as an activist, though, until my city passed a set of anti-loitering and panhandling laws. It seems the powerful business interests in town didn't want the tourists scared away by the street people. Through Sam, who regularly "camps out" in the alley beside my office building, I met several homeless folks and a variety of people from social service agencies and good samaritan groups serving them. What was missing was an interest from the private sector.

I began talking to my colleagues at work and in my business associations. I was surprised to find several people who wanted to get involved, but didn't know how. Together we started the Shelter Committee, a vehicle for exploring the root causes of the growing problem of homelessness in our community. Our research plus our credibility allowed us to be a link between the various groups addressing the needs of the homeless and those making the public policies—and, of course, with the homeless themselves, who were always included in our discussions.

A year of active coalition building resulted in a sharp increase in available low-cost housing, a special fund for preventing families from losing their homes, and the repeal of the more odious anti-homeless laws. There are still too many people with no place to call home, but at least we've made a start.

RESOURCE GUIDE

Check within your local community for groups involved in the social justice, change, and activist topics that interest you. Here are some suggestions:

PROGRAMS AND ORGANIZATIONS

AMNESTY INTERNATIONAL

Worldwide campaigning movement to promote human rights. AI and its members take action to free prisoners of conscience; ensure fair and prompt trials for political prisoners; abolish the death penalty, torture, and other cruel treatment of prisoners; and end political killings and "disappearances."

NEW YORK, NY; PHONE: 212-807-8400;
E-MAIL: admin-us@aiusa.org; WEB SITE: www.aiusa.org

THE INSTITUTE FOR PEACE AND JUSTICE

An independent, interfaith, nonprofit organization responding to war, racism, and global economic injustice, helping people find alternatives that incorporate justice and reconciliation into an active quest for peace in everyday lives.

ST. LOUIS, MO; PHONE: 314-533-4445; FAX: 314-715-6455;
E-MAIL: ipj@ipj-ppj.org; WEB SITE: www.ipj-ppj.org

PEACE ACTION

A national membership, grassroots peace and disarmament organization. Peace Action is committed to the abolition of nuclear weapons, redirection of excessive Pentagon spending, an end to global weapon sales, and non-military resolutions to international conflicts.

WASHINGTON, DC; PHONE: 202-862-9740; FAX: 202-862-9762;
E-MAIL: jbridgman@peace-action.org;
WEB SITE: www. peace-action.org

BOOKS, TAPES, VIDEOS

The Art of Peace: Nobel Peace Laureates Discuss Human Rights, Conflict and Reconciliation. Jeffrey Hopkins and Jose Ramos Horta, eds. Snow Lion Publications, 2000.

Making a Just Peace: Human Rights and Domination Systems. C. Dale White. Abindgon Press, 1998.

A Peace Reader: Essential Readings on War, Justice, Non-Violence, and World Order. Joseph J. Fahey and Richard Armonstrong, eds. Paulist Press, 1992.

Teaching for Social Justice. William Ayers, et al, eds. New Press, 1998.

WEB SITES

DERECHOS HUMAN RIGHTS

Internet-based human rights organization. Works for the promotion and respect of human rights all over the world, for the right to privacy and against impunity for human rights violators.

www.derechos.org

PEACE AND ANTI-WAR MOVEMENT SITES

In the run-up to the war in Iraq, a number of web sites helped galvanize, organize and educate the fast-growing constituency against the war. Many are still active. These include:

www.codepink4peace.org
www.patriotsforpeace.org
www.moveon.org
www.unitedforpeace.org
www.winwithoutwar.org

PEACENET

Online directory of Peacenet organizations. Web site includes action alerts, headline news, links to other progressive IGC sites, advocacy tips, discussions, and a documents database with search command.

www.igc.org/igc/gateway

PEACEWEB

A Quaker Web page on peace and social concerns. Online resources for economy/justice, children and peace, development, Quakers and the UN, and movies with a conscience.

www.web.net/~peaceweb

20/20 VISION

Makes grassroots activism simple for busy people with information for twenty-minute actions to make a difference.

www.2020vision.org

UNITED NATIONS

Describes United Nations work for human rights; includes text of the UN Declaration of Human Rights.

www.un.org/rights

WebActive

Gives the Internet an effective tool for progressive activism. Features progressive news links and online events.

www.webactive.com

Keywords to explore through your computer search engine: *social justice, peace and justice, social change, social action, activism*

NINE

PEACE & NONVIOLENCE
Lay Down Your Sword and Shield

*I believe that the basic nature of human beings is gentle
and compassionate. It is therefore in our own interest
to encourage that nature, to make it live within us, to
leave room for it to develop. If on the contrary we use
violence, it is as if we voluntarily obstruct the positive
side of human nature and prevent its evolution.*

—HIS HOLINESS THE DALAI LAMA

Nonviolence is a concept that is easily misunderstood. Many
people associate it with being soft, passive, or submissive. In
fact, nonviolence is an active, vibrant commitment to respect
life in all that we do. It is a commitment to life-enhancing rather than
life-depleting behavior. Violence is about force, hurting, and demeaning. Nonviolence is about respect, loving, and supporting.

Nonviolence can be understood along a wide continuum. At one
end is the individual desire to avoid harming others in body, mind, and
spirit. At the other is a lifelong commitment to nonviolent action for

peace and justice for all the peoples of the world. To build a culture of peace, we must align ourselves somewhere on that continuum, for nothing destroys the fabric of peace faster than violence in any form.

73 UNDERSTAND THE HYPNOTIC EFFECT OF VIOLENCE

We live in a culture of violence. Violence has become a way of life for us. We are so used to this that we hardly notice anymore how much violence permeates what we see, hear, and experience in our daily world.

Because we have adapted to violence as a norm, we have become lethargic and unresponsive to it. You might say we are under some hypnotic effect. If we stopped and thought about it, we might say that all that violence is bad for us, and we would feel like doing something to change things. But we don't stop and think about it; we act as if it's not a problem, as if it is "just how things are," or we shake our heads and think how bad it is, but do nothing.

We collude, or go along with the culture of violence not because we necessarily agree with it, but because it's easier to do nothing. Our response-ability becomes dulled.

- Watch your reaction to how violence is portrayed in:

   Primetime television shows

   Conventional children's cartoons

   News broadcasts

   Newspapers and magazines

   What do you notice?

- Watch your reaction to how violence is present (subtly or directly) in our public discourse on such issues as:

   Abortion

   Death penalty

   Crime

   Race

   Political campaigns

   What do you notice?

• Watch your reaction to the role of violence in sports. What do you notice?

• Watch your reaction to violent video games. Do you yourself play them? Do your children, or children of friends? What do you notice?

• What can you do, what positive action can you take, to lessen the acceptability of violence in our culture? What keeps you from doing it?

74 TAKE A SELF-TEST ON NONVIOLENCE

Nonviolence is not always a clear-cut choice. There are many ambiguities, conditions, and circumstances that affect us when we think about our commitment to nonviolence. Here is a simple self-test that will give you more information about your own relation to nonviolence. There are no right or wrong, good or bad answers—simply a fuller picture of where you stand.

NONVIOLENCE SELF-TEST

1 Rate each of the items below with numbers from the following scale: 1—I strongly disagree.   2—I disagree.   3—I agree.
4—I agree strongly.   5—I'm not sure what I believe.

____ 1 Violence is never justified, under any condition.

____ 2 Violence can be justified in the following circumstances:

____ To protect a stranger.

____ To protect a loved one.

____ To protect property.

____ To stop a crime from being committed.

____ To stop harm being done to the environment.

____ To protest injustice.

____ To protest or promote issues that I feel strongly about.

____ Other (Please specify).

____ 3 There may be times when war is necessary to stop a larger evil.

____ **4** I myself would fight in a war if I believed it was a "just" war.

____ **5** I myself would never take up arms in a war, under any circumstances.

____ **6** Words can be just as violent as action.

____ **7** Nonviolence is, for me:

    ____ An important spiritual value.

    ____ An important secular, moral principle.

    ____ A pragmatic choice for effective social change.

____ **8** I would take part in nonviolent action campaigns for a cause I believed in.

____ **9** I would be willing to be arrested in a nonviolent action campaign for a cause I believed in.

____ **10** I would be willing to undergo physical harm (tear gas, water hose, beating, pepper spray) in a nonviolent action campaign for a cause I believed in.

2 Now look at all the questions for which you answered 1 or 2, indicating disagreement. Does the pattern tell you anything about yourself?

3 Look at all the questions for which you answered 3 or 4, indicating agreement. What does the pattern suggest? Look at all the questions for which you answered 5, indicating ambivalence or lack of clarity. What do you notice?

4 Share this test with other people (family, friends, colleagues, social groups), and talk together about the results and the questions raised by those results.

75 DO A NONVIOLENCE INVENTORY OF YOUR HOME AND FAMILY

There are many situations in our daily lives at home with family where the choice for violence or nonviolence is present. Some of these are obvious, some less so.

Whereas the self-test referred to your beliefs, this inventory involves things that you actually do. Again, there is no right or wrong, good or bad response. An honest assessment of your lifestyle may give you useful information about how you choose to live your values.

NONVIOLENCE INVENTORY

Rate the frequency of each of the actions following with numbers from the following scale. 1—Never 2—Rarely 3—Sometimes 4—Often 5—Always

In my household I/we:

____ 1 Use hitting (slapping, spanking) for punishment of children.

____ 2 Use shaming and blaming words to correct bad behavior.

3 Have rules or strong norms against hitting (or other forms of hurting)

____ Children

____ Adults

____ Animals

____ 4 Enjoy watching television shows about murder, crime, or other depictions of violence.

____ 5 Enjoy watching action, suspense, or horror movies.

____ 6 Own a gun.

____ 7 Allow toy weapons, war toys, and violent play-acting.

____ 8 Enjoy playing violent video games.

____ 9 Kill bugs and other pests found inside or outside the house.

____ 10 Capture bugs found inside the house and release them outside.

____ 11 Have angry fights, using accusations, blame, belittling, or mean words.

____ 12 Talk about any of these things.

What did you learn from this inventory? What, if anything, will you do differently as a result of it?

76   PRACTICE NONVIOLENT COMMUNICATION

Violence is not limited to physical activity. Words can hurt too. Even our nonverbal communication—looks, facial expressions, body postures—can convey harmful messages.

Embracing nonviolence requires paying attention to the total picture of our communication and replacing patterns that hurt with new patterns that show love, respect, and encouragement.

• Do a negative language fast. Pick a reasonable period of time (a day, a week) and commit yourself to eliminating all words of negativity from your vocabulary during that period. Negative language includes put-downs, blaming or shaming words (*should* or *shouldn't*), belittling words, disempowering words (*can't*), labels, gossip, or other ways of speaking to yourself or to others that are mean-spirited.

• Replace put-downs with positive encouragement. Put-downs are ways of making someone else feel small, unworthy, or unlovable. Positive encouragement helps people stretch and grow and feel capable and lovable. For instance, instead of, "You are so stupid," say, "I know you can do it; try again."

• Replace "you" statements with "I" statements. "You" statements are when we wag our finger at someone and tell them what to do or what's wrong with them. Most people feel defensive when they hear a "you" statement. "I" statements keep us on the only subject about which we can really know anything, which is our own experience. For instance, instead of, "You make me so mad!" say, "I feel angry when you do that, and I want you to stop!"

• Replace sneers with smiles; a rolling of the eyes or raised eyebrow with direct and friendly eye contact; a look of boredom with a look of interest. See how this changes the quality of the communication—and the relationship.

77   SOFTEN YOUR DEFENSES

Defensiveness is a natural reaction to having been hurt. We learn to defend ourselves against rejection, to protect our hearts against pain. We want to justify our actions and beliefs and guard ourselves from whatever we find frightening.

The shield is the other side of the sword. When we shield ourselves, we tighten up. This makes us more likely to attract attack and unable to receive whatever good energy is coming our way. The more defended we are, the less able we are to let our hearts open in love and peace.

- First step, always, is just to be aware. Pay attention to when and how you feel defensive. What happens in your body? In your mind? In your heart?

- Ask what you are protecting yourself from. Can you actually stop whatever it is you are afraid of from happening?

- Experiment with acting "as if." For instance, when you feel defensive, act "as if" you felt totally open and at ease, with nothing to defend against. If you are suspicious, act "as if" you were totally trusting. If you are distrustful, act "as if" it's okay to trust. What do you notice?

- Notice the defenses that others put up toward you. How does that feel? What could you do to provide reassurance that you won't hurt them?

78   ENCOURAGE NONVIOLENT SOLUTIONS TO CONFLICTS

Conflict is a normal part of human interaction. It can even be a positive experience, because it gives us the opportunity to grow greater love, kindness, and compassion in our relationships. It also helps us learn how to solve problems effectively.

Unfortunately, our society has become used to moving rapidly to violence—of language and action—to resolve our conflicts. We haven't learned how to manage low-level disputes and keep them from escalating into something more dangerous and explosive. When we commit to the nonviolent resolution of conflict, we commit to peace.

- Develop an internal escalation meter. Learn to sense when a simple difference of opinion or desire moves out of the cool zone (where things seem quite manageable) and into the hot zone (where emotions run high and danger looms). Find ways to keep your disputes in the cool zone.

• Practice "fair fighting." Nonviolence doesn't mean to avoid conflicts. It simply means to move through them in a clean way, without verbal or physical attacks, to find a peaceful and empowering resolution. The rules of a fair fight are:

1 Each party has a right to dignity and respect.

2 The process will be a win-win effort so that each party gets their basic needs and interests satisfied.

3 The outcome will leave people feeling better about themselves and each other.

• Become an expert in negotiation. Read books, take classes, practice negotiation at home, work, and play. Share what you learn about negotiation with your friends, family, and colleagues. Good negotiation skills help promote fair fighting.

• Become an advocate for nonviolent conflict resolution. Actively promote programs of nonviolent conflict resolution in schools, places of worship, the workplace, the community commons, prisons, health programs, government, the courts. Celebrate the success stories from these programs as publicly as possible.

79 PROMOTE NONVIOLENCE IN THE MEDIA

Our media outlets currently provide our greatest exposure to violence as a way of life. The print media routinely report on wars, massacres, and murders in all their grisly details. Television news shows provide graphic details of public mayhem. We watch real-time bombing of cities and towns around the world. TV talk shows provoke passions and encourage people to attack each other on stage. The public sits riveted.

Meanwhile, our television shows sensationalize the seamy side of life. Tales of brutal homicides, twisted serial killers, terrorist attacks, and end-of-the-world destruction scenarios are blockbuster action hits. Our popular music fills the airwaves with nasty language about women, and about sex as a form of conquest. Our children get educated in the thousands of different ways to kill poor Coyote.

Violence is glamorized and glorified in the media to the point that we have become desensitized to what it really is. It doesn't have to be this way.

· Insist on equal time for nonviolent stories. Editors and filmmakers will say that violence sells because it is so exciting. Find and promote stories of equally high drama involving nonviolent solutions to difficult situations. Lobby hard with local and national media to include them.

· Protest the level of violence in the media. Arrange a community meeting of concerned citizens with the editor of your local newspaper. Organize a boycott of a movie theater showing a particularly gruesome film. Spearhead an e-mail campaign to flood the major networks with complaints about their lopsided programming.

· Talk with children, parents, teachers, and other community members and leaders about the media messages on violence. What do people see and hear and take away from that exposure? How do they make sense of it? Encourage regular family conversations as well as public dialogue on the subject.

· Set limits. Draw your own line about what you will expose yourself to and what you will buy and allow in your home. Encourage your friends and colleagues to do the same.

80 CELEBRATE THE HEROES AND HEROINES OF NONVIOLENCE

We have many inspiring role models of nonviolence. Mahatma Gandhi, Rev. Martin Luther King, Jr., Mother Teresa, His Holiness the Dalai Lama, and Nelson Mandela are giants in our times. These people have demonstrated, with their own lives, the miracle and mystery of nonviolent action to touch our souls and change the world.

When we study the writings and the acts of these moral figures, we absorb their wisdom and strengthen our own longing for lives of love and peace in action. They express the ideal that is our highest potential and desire. The more we learn from them, the more like them we become.

• Pick your own role model. Find a hero or heroine of nonviolence who touches something deep in you. While the people mentioned here are perhaps the best known, there are many other figures of current or historical interest who are equally courageous and inspiring. With a little exploration, you can find them.

• Study the literature. Read the writings of your favorite hero or heroine and of other nonviolent giants. Memorize quotes that especially speak to you. Share your favorite passages with friends and family.

• Fill your space with inspirational material. Make posters of your favorite quotes. Find pictures of your hero. Put them every-where—over your bed, on the refrigerator, on the wall at work or school.

• Imagine you and your heroine are one. Put yourself in her shoes during one of her most inspiring or challenging moments. Can you feel how she might have felt? When you face a moment of testing in your own life, think what she would do in that situation.

• Celebrate the birthdays, anniversaries, or other special events associated with your hero or heroine. Throw a party in their honor. Applaud their legacy.

81   ENGAGE IN NONVIOLENT ACTION FOR A CAUSE YOU BELIEVE IN

Nonviolence can be path for social change as well as a moral value and a way of life. Dedicated individuals or groups practicing non-violent protest or other forms of persuasion can, literally, change the world. In the twentieth century alone, nonviolent action brought down empires, overturned governments, and ended wars.

Nonviolent action is a way for individuals to show solidarity for people who are oppressed. It is a way to witness for the kind of world we believe in. It is a way to act locally while thinking globally, putting our highest values and ideals into constructive and positive practice. It gives us a chance to walk our talk.

· Pick a cause that touches you. Make a commitment to be actively involved in promoting it—nonviolently.

· Educate yourself. Study the issue carefully, understand the parties involved and the whole range of views before you move to action. Know what's important to you about this cause, and why.

· Find organizations and other individuals working nonviolently for this cause. Learn about their activities. Join with them. Be clear about your goals. Strategize the best kind of action to achieve that goal.

· Stand up for what you believe through a variety of actions, including:

Marches

Prayer vigils

Peaceful demonstrations

Teach-ins

Walkouts

Boycotts

Symbolic public acts

· Get trained in nonviolent action and civil disobedience. Many organizations provide such training (see the Resource Guide; look on the Web).

· Participate in a civil disobedience initiative. Use your personal power of love and the power of collective action to confront injustice or repression. Be prepared to endure the sanctions and consequences of your stance.

· Stand in solidarity with nonviolent actions. If you can't, for whatever reason, participate yourself, support those who do. Give money, make posters, cheer from the sidelines, make bail, provide transportation, serve coffee. Take even the smallest step to make a difference.

REVIEW

Practice the Four Principles of Peace and Nonviolence

COMMUNITY
Build a support system for reducing
violence and promoting nonviolence in our media.

COOPERATION
Work with people of like mind to confront
societal wrongs through nonviolent action.

NONVIOLENCE
Commit to nonviolence as a way of life.

WITNESS
Stand up for what you believe in—live the active power of love.

THE BIRTH OF A NONVIOLENT WARRIOR

A commitment to nonviolence grows through testing. When faced with a moment of choice, which way will we go? Will our fear cause us to run away, or our adrenaline cause us to fight? This story tells of such a moment for one young woman.

When groups started forming on my college campus in preparation for the IMF-World Bank demonstrations in Washington, D. C., I attended my first social action meeting. I learned about the inequities of globalization, but most important, I was trained in nonviolent social action.

On the streets of Washington, all was chaos. Different groups were demonstrating in different ways, and the police were unpredictable. I saw a lot of people get hurt.

One incident in particular stands out. A few of us were trying to find the rest of our team, having become separated in the confusion. As we turned a corner, suddenly there was a group of police in full riot gear. We stopped, and stood quietly. Someone whispered a reminder to stay calm and to recall that our issue was not with the police but with the World Bank.

The police started toward us menacingly, shields raised. I was so scared I wanted to run. But the words of my training came back to me: "The purpose is to witness your love for all humanity." In that moment, I realized that "all humanity"included not just the poor in the developing world who, I thought, were being hurt by World Bank and IMF policies, but the police right in front of me, who were just doing their job as best they could.

I stood straighter, and let that love for all humanity come through my eyes, as I looked directly at the policeman in front of me. The others in my group must have been doing something similar, because the police stopped just a couple of feet away from us, lowered their shields, and asked where we were headed. They escorted us safely around a noisy crowd so we could rejoin our group.

I realized later how easily I could have become argumentative and confrontational in that moment, seeing those policemen as "the enemy."

But by staying clear about my purpose for being there, and by including the police in that purpose, I came to understand the true power of nonviolent action.

RESOURCE GUIDE

Check within your local community for programs of nonviolent action or training, for nonviolent communication workshops, or for events honoring nonviolent heroes and heroines. Here are some suggestions:

PROGRAMS AND ORGANIZATIONS

ALTERNATIVES TO VIOLENCE PROGRAM (AVP)

Dedicated to reducing the level of violence in our society, focusing especially on schools, communities, and prisons. A nationwide and worldwide association of volunteer groups offering experiential workshops teaching the same nonviolent skills and techniques used by Mohandas Gandhi and the Rev. Martin Luther King, Jr.

SYRACUSE, NY; PHONE: 713-747-9999;
E-MAIL: avp@avpusa.org; WEB SITE: www.avpusa.org

THE FELLOWSHIP OF RECONCILIATION

An interfaith organization committed to active nonviolence as a transforming way of life and as a means of radical change. FOR educates, trains, builds coalitions, and engages in nonviolent and compassionate actions locally, nationally, and globally. Branches and affiliates in 40 countries.

NYACK, NY; PHONE: 845-358-4601; FAX: 845-358-4924;
E-MAIL: for@forusa.org; WEB SITE: www.forusa.org

THE MARTIN LUTHER KING, JR. CENTER
FOR NONVIOLENT SOCIAL CHANGE, INC

Serves as the national and international clearing house for officially sanctioned King programs and products. Information on King Holiday, community involvement, King's words and philosophy.

ATLANTA, GA; PHONE: 404-526-8900
E-MAIL: information@thekingcenter.org;
WEB SITE: www.thekingcenter.com

TRAINING FOR CHANGE

Spreads the skills of democratic, nonviolent social change. Leads workshops for nonviolent activists to help groups stand up for justice, peace, and environmental harmony.

PHILADELPHIA, PA; PHONE: 215-729-7458; FAX: 215-729-1910;
E-MAIL: peacelearn@igc.org; WEB SITE: www.TrainingForChange.org

WAR RESISTERS LEAGUE

Uses methods ranging from education to demonstrations to lobbying to nonviolent direct action—at all times trying to see those we oppose not as enemies, but as sisters and brothers. Nonviolent activist peace calendar.

NEW YORK, NY; PHONE: 212-228-0450; FAX: 212-228-6193;
E-MAIL: wrl@igc.org; WEB SITE: www.warresisters.org

BOOKS, TAPES, VIDEOS

Force More Powerful: A Century of Nonviolent Conflict. Video; PBS documentary showing how, during a century of extreme violence, millions chose to battle brutality and oppression with nonviolent weapons—and won. Available online at www.pbs.org/weta/forcemorepowerful/

Gandhi on Non-Violence: Selected Texts from Gandhi's Non-Violence in Peace and War. Mahatma Gandhi. Thomas Merton, ed. New Directions Publishing Co., 1968.

Love in Action: Writings on Nonviolent Social Change. Thich Nhat Hanh. Parallax Press, 1993.

Martin Luther King, Jr.: Nonviolent Strategies and Tactics for Social Change. John J. Ansbro. Madison Books, Inc., 2000.

Nonviolent Communication: A Language of Compassion. Marshall Rosenberg. Puddle Dancer Press, 1999.

Peace Is the Way: Writings on Nonviolence from the Fellowship of Reconciliation. Walter Wink, ed. Introduction by Richard Deats. Fellowship of Reconciliation, 2000.

WEB SITES

THE NONVIOLENCE WEB

Access to dozens of U.S.-based peace groups. Articles and resources, nationally and internationally organized efforts to pursue nonviolent solutions to today's problems.

www.nonviolence.org

Keywords to explore through your computer search engine: *nonviolence, violence prevention, anti-violence, alternatives to violence, pacifism, Gandhi, Martin Luther King, Jr.*

TEN

WORLD PEACE

Let There Be Peace on Earth. . . .

We belong to each other.
—MOTHER TERESA

stronauts have noticed that the Earth's national political boundaries are invisible from space. We all share the same home. What happens in Central Asia or Central America affects our lives in America. An ethnic clash far away may seem like a distant event, but it can create refugees who then destablize the social environment of other countries; it can strengthen the hand of arms dealers and drug dealers who are searching for new markets; it can hurt the economy of a whole region, which has implications for our local economy.

A culture of peace involves us in curiosity about the state of peace everywhere. It engages us in action and commitment, to promote peace for the whole family of life on Earth. In the global village of the twenty-first century, we cannot afford to live in isolation. The whole world is our back yard, and world peace is the dream we are creating together.

82   TAKE AN INTEREST IN WORLD AFFAIRS

Modern communication technology has brought the world into our living rooms. We can see what's happening on every continent. Some people turn off to this flow of information. It may seem like too much suffering, too complicated a picture of situations we don't understand in places that feel foreign to us.

We can turn away, or we can turn toward what's happening around the world. When we turn toward it, we discover that what may appear as an endless progression of war, famine, corruption, and political intrigue is actually an exciting story of humanity addressing its challenges as best it can. Each of us is an actor, director, script-writer, and audience for this rich and inspiring drama.

• Read about world affairs. Read local and national newspapers and news magazines. Subscribe to specialized information sources: journals, news services on the Web, international papers. Read about international political news, business news, even the weather!

• Learn about world affairs from television. Watch news shows, international broadcasts, and special reports on international issues.

• Follow one particular theme—famine, water, education of girls, overpopulation, ethnic warfare, elections in emerging nations, micro-credit programs, small arms sales. Become knowledgeable about the issue and how it is being addressed in various countries. What is successful? What is not?

• Learn about the foreign policy arm of your own government. Explore how the U.S. State Department operates; find out about the U.S. Agency for International Development (USAID) and the U.S. Information Agency (USIA).

- Educate yourself about international bodies: The United Nations and its related agencies; regional organizations like the Organization of American States (OAS); intergovernmental institutions like the World Bank or the International Monetary Fund; and international nongovernmental organizations such as CARE, Doctors Without Borders, or Save the Children.

83 ADOPT ONE PLACE IN THE WORLD AS YOUR SPECIAL CONCERN

Every place in the world is struggling with something. Find a situation where there is a meeting point between an issue you are interested in and a place that calls your attention.

Being attentive to one situation allows you to go deeply with your expertise, your commitment, and your caring for peace. It gives you a focus for understanding yourself as a citizen of the world and an agent of peace.

- Inform yourself. Find out all you can about your selected spot: keep up with the news; look at related Web sites; contact the country's embassy; read novels, poetry, travelogues, and political commentary about the place; learn about the culture.

- Get a pen pal. Correspond with someone who lives there, by mail or e-mail. Get their views on the situation. Let them explain to you the range of local perspectives, which may be different from yours as an outsider.

- Talk to people who have been there. Find people who went as tourists, as peace or development workers, or on business. Listen to their stories; use their experiences to round out your own understanding.

- Go there. Go visit your pen pal. Find an organization that welcomes volunteers. Sign on for a short-term consulting job with an international organization working there. Just get on a plane and arrive; be a tourist.

- Host people from that country in your home. Invite your pen pal. Host an exchange student, or someone traveling for business, fundraising, or medical treatment.

84 LET YOUR HEART BREAK WITH THE SUFFERING

Sometimes, we hold ourselves back from involvement in world affairs because of the intense suffering we see. How can we bear to deal with the reality of thousands of starving children? Raped women? Whole villages massacred?

Trying to hold the suffering away by staying away will not help. Only when you face squarely into the suffering and allow your heart to break with compassion can you truly stand in solidarity with the victims of violence. Only when your heart is open can you truly serve.

• Relax your defenses. When you focus on a situation in the world that is painful, notice the different ways you defend yourself against feeling that hurt. Now gently relax that protective stance. Let the pain in, a bit at a time. Breathe deeply.

• Weep for the suffering. When you open your heart and let in the suffering of the world, a natural response is to be sad. If tears come, let them come; don't try to stop them. If it feels like your heart is breaking, that is a good sign. It means you are making room for more caring.

• Feel compassion. Compassion is not pity or sympathy but a heartfelt desire that the suffering of others might be eased. Hold the victims of violence and disaster in a compassionate embrace in your heart; hold the perpetrators also, for they too are victims of violence.

• Feel loving kindness. Loving kindness is the heartfelt desire that others might live with peace, freedom, and joy. Hold the victims of violence and disaster in an embrace of loving kindness in your heart.

• Be present without having to fix it. Sometimes, when we see people hurting, we think we must make it all better. We cannot fix the pain of the world, but when we let ourselves be fully present to it we give the gift of witness.

85   SUPPORT ORGANIZATIONS DOING INTERNATIONAL PEACE WORK

Many organizations exist specifically to work for peace in the world. Some are part of the UN system; some are connected to governments or universities or religious institutions; some are completely independent.

Each organization has its own unique mission. Some work at the highest political levels, seeking formal peace agreements. Others work behind the scenes, to foster dialogue and generate creative options for resolution. Still others work at the grassroots level, building bridges of understanding or working for change in the educational system or the media.

These organizations need help. Many of them depend on money from individuals like yourself to keep going. Others require a broad base of support through caring, engaged members.

• Find out who's doing what. Ask around your network of friends and colleagues to learn about specific organizations, or check the Resource Guide provided at the end of the chapter.

• Become a member. Find an organization that speaks to you, and join up. Pay dues. Read their newsletters and other materials. Tell your friends about them.

• Become a volunteer. Some organizations are set up to use volunteers in their offices or in the field where their programs are. Seek out the best fit for your skills and interests with what's needed.

• Be a cheerleader. Find organizations you like, and actively cheer them on. Write encouraging notes, congratulate them on a job well done, offer to put them in touch with resources that you think might be useful to them.

• Contribute money. These organizations all need money; rarely do they have enough to meet the incredible need. Even a small check can be a great gift. Or, save your petty cash or spare change over several months and send a bigger check. Better yet, pick one or more organizations and make it the primary recipient of your charitable giving.

86 SUPPORT INTERNATIONAL AID AGENCIES

Relief and humanitarian organizations are a little bit different from peacemaking groups. These agencies are concerned with the basics of human life: food, shelter, water, education, and health. They are on the scene when disaster hits, saving lives.

Increasingly, these organizations are staying long after the flood or earthquake or civil war, supporting the long-term development needs of the people so that they can sustain themselves over time. More and more, this is overlapping with peace work. The two depend on each other. Peace cannot prevail when people are hungry; people cannot grow a strong economy when there is war.

- Educate yourself. Learn what agencies exist, what they are doing, what the needs are, what the obstacles are, and what the success stories are.

- Pick one or two agencies whose work particularly touches your heart. Support them financially, and in any other way you can.

- Sponsor a child, or a child's education, somewhere in the world.

- Respond to emergency appeals when a natural disaster strikes. Stay involved after the peak of the emergency passes.

- Offer your services in an emergency if you have a specialized skill.

- Give blood. Give clothes. Give food. Give time.

- Send prayers. Send love. Send money.

87 GET INVOLVED AT YOUR PLACE OF WORSHIP

Your place of worship is a good place to get involved in programs that take the international perspective. Most faith traditions put a high value on issues of peace and development. It is good to work with others who share your values.

Another advantage to working from your place of worship is that it helps build community. Through your own local congregation, and also through the larger network of your parent body, you are able to be part of a much larger mission.

• Find out if your church, synagogue, temple, mosque, or other place of worship has any programs for international work. They may participate in aid and relief, education, social and economic development, social justice, or peacebuilding projects.

• Go to the meetings of these projects. Find out what's happening. Sense where you are drawn.

• Support the initiative(s) you are drawn to with your time, your skills, and your money.

• If the program you want doesn't exist, start it. Ask your clergy person for help. Talk to other members of your faith community to find like-minded people.

• Travel with a group from your place of worship on a trip they are taking. Work to help organize the travel arrangements. Host someone coming from out of town who is involved with this project.

• Organize study groups, film showings, book readings, lectures, and other events to educate your team and your wider community on the issues you are concerned with.

• Give a guest sermon or speak at some special event about your international activities.

88   TRAVEL ON A PEACE MISSION

Many organizations take teams of peacebuilders to troubled places where an international presence can be especially helpful. Where people are oppressed and vulnerable, international witnesses from other countries can serve as a ray of hope, provide doorways for dialogue, or be a deterrent to further violence.

These peace missions are usually volunteer in nature. They may provide observers to important functions, like election monitoring. They may gather information, such as data on human rights abuses. They may provide a safe presence for refugees trying to return to their homes. Or they may do important work in the community— physical labor or community organizing.

• Find the peace mission that best fits your interests. Check it out thoroughly. Talk to people who have participated. Where does their money come from? Make sure there is an experienced team leader.

• Know what is expected of you. How long will you stay? How much will it cost you, and what does that cover? What will happen if you get sick? Will you be alone or with a team? What dangers might you face?

• Get the training you need. Good intentions are not enough. You need to know exactly what your job entails—and what it doesn't. You need to be sure you have the right skills to accomplish your task, so that you will not inadvertently cause harm to the people you are trying to help.

• Request orientation assistance. What should you study before you go? How much of the language should you know? What should you be especially alert to?

• Request debriefing assistance. What will happen when you get back? Will you be asked to speak publicly or to write about your experience? Will there be someone to help you make sense of your experience and integrate it?

89 BECOME INVOLVED WITH REFUGEES IN YOUR TOWN

These days, you don't have to go far away to work for planetary peace; sometimes the world comes to you. Many of today's conflicts have created masses of refugees, people fleeing the dangers of their own countries, seeking safety elsewhere.

Refugees from war-torn societies are present throughout the United States. They may arrive with little or no knowledge of English, and with varying degrees of comfort with the life and culture of America. They may have suffered grave trauma, or milder economic and social displacement.

• Discover who are the main refugee groups in your community. Find out about their circumstances. How many are there; why did they leave their homes; how long have they been here; how have they adjusted?

• Explore existing programs. Find out what services are already provided and by whom, and what is still needed.

• Take the time to build trust. Remember, you are a stranger to them, just as they may seem "foreign" to you. They may be culturally sensitive to receiving help, or may have experiences that make it hard for them to trust outsiders. Go slowly. Have patience.

• Attend events. Gradually get to know the people by participating in their activities. Go to meetings to discuss refugee-related issues; attend a cultural celebration that is open to the public; be an observer during some event where services are delivered by a church group or city department.

• Help a refugee family get settled, learn how to move around town (shop, use unfamiliar appliances, enroll children in school), find the social services they need.

• Get involved in dialogue. Many refugee communities bring with them the same hostilities that caused the problems back home. Help build bridges between the factions. Start by working with existing organizations who do this. Eventually become a facilitator yourself.

90   PRACTICE CITIZEN DIPLOMACY

These days, informal, citizen-to-citizen diplomacy is an important part of any peace process. Remember that the formal, official peace process managed by the UN or some other official body will only deal with legal and political matters. It will not reach the people, to affect what is in their hearts and minds. This can only be done on a person-to-person basis.

Likewise, building strong relationships with outside groups can provide trust, hope, and a sense of support to people who may be struggling. Knowing that someone else cares and that resources are available can be the fuel that keeps people going through the hard times.

• Read "Guidelines to Newcomers to Track Two Diplomacy" (see the Resource Guide). This article will help you know what to expect and how to act so that you can do the most good and the least harm.

• Join or start a sister cities program. This is where your town joins with a city of approximately the same size somewhere in the world where you want to build links. Participate in administering the program and in any trips or exchanges that occur.

• Be or host an exchange student. Personal relationships developed while staying in someone's home can last for years and can be doorways to a whole network of caring relationships and associations.

• Join an existing citizen-diplomacy project. This may be in any area: business, education, religion, media, arts, or sports. In these projects, you have the opportunity to make an offering of your special skills, to follow your interests, or just to build bridges of friendship and mutual understanding.

REVIEW

Practice the Four Principles of Peace on Earth

COMMUNITY
Let the world into your life; decide to personally
be part of the solution to world problems.

COOPERATION
Work with others to provide support and solidarity
for those who are hurt by war and other disasters.

NONVIOLENCE
Respect the dignity of those who are vulnerable;
prepare yourself so that your actions will do no harm.

WITNESS
Open your heart to the suffering of the
world, and pour love into the wounds.

DO SOMETHING!

Within the global community, we have access to information about wars far away. Often we are touched by the suffering of war victims, but few of us are prepared to do anything concrete about it. In this story, an American child started a process for her community to make a difference.

Ishmet B. was three days old when he was driven from his burning home in Kosovo. His terrified father, his exhausted mother, and his traumatized brother, Adem, welcomed him into a chaotic world. He spent his first three months in a tiny tent in a Macedonian refugee camp, listening to his crying brother and sensing the shock and pain of his parents. His family had lost their home, their business, and possibly their family. His only uncle was in a Serbian prison.

Around the time that Ishmet was born, Mari, a twelve-year-old girl from the beautiful village of Danville (population 2,000) in Vermont, asked her parents to "Do something!" when she saw a picture of refugees on the cover of *Newsweek*. Three months later, Mari's and Ishmet's families were living together, and many in the Danville community were surrounding the B.'s with a blanket of love and practical support. An ecumenical group, prompted by Mari and others, had arranged to "Do something!"

Today, Ishmet's family is living in a nice apartment near Danville. The fear has disappeared from his parents' faces. His brother is a happy, confident little boy. The B.'s still have worries, and they struggle to make ends meet with jobs that pay too little. They miss their families and their home, but they have each other, and they have friends like Mari. For now, they have enough.

RESOURCE GUIDE

Check within your local community for sister city or citizen exchange programs, world affairs events, and refugee resettlement projects. Here are some suggestions:

PROGRAMS AND ORGANIZATIONS

AMERICAN INTERCULTURAL STUDENT EXCHANGE

Dedicated to fostering increased international understanding through worldwide intercultural learning and living experiences. AISE gives high school students from 27 countries the opportunity to live in the United States as members of the local community; offers reciprocal programs for American students.

LAJOLLA, CA; PHONE: 858-459-9761 OR 1-800-SIBLING; FAX: 858-459-5301; E-MAIL: aise.usa@worldnet.att.net; WEB SITE: www.aise.com

CARE

One of the world's largest private international relief and development organizations. CARE reaches out to people whose lives are devastated by humanitarian emergencies or who are struggling each day in poor communities to survive and improve their lives.

ATLANTA, GA; PHONE: 404-681-2552; E-MAIL: info@care.org; WEB SITE: www.care.org

INSTITUTE FOR MULTI-TRACK DIPLOMACY

Promotes a transformative, systems approach to peace in places of deep-rooted conflict around the world. IMTD helps people from all sectors of society find ways to step forward as responsible peace-builders in their communities.

ARLINGTON, VA; PHONE: 703-528-3863; FAX: 703-528-5776; E-MAIL: imtd@imtd.org; WEB SITE: www.imtd.org

PEACE BRIGADES INTERNATIONAL

A grassroots organization that explores and implements nonviolent approaches to peacekeeping and defending human rights. When invited, sends teams of international volunteers into areas of conflict to deter violence and promote active nonviolence through accompaniment, peace education, and conflict analysis and observation.

OAKLAND, CA; PHONE: 510-663-2362; FAX: 510-663-2364;
E-MAIL: pbiusa@agc.org; WEB SITE: www.peacebrigades.org

WITNESS FOR PEACE

A politically independent, grassroots organization committed to nonviolence and led by faith and conscience. Seeks to support peace, justice, and sustainable economies in the Americas by changing U.S. policies and corporate practices that contribute to poverty and oppression in Latin America and the Caribbean.

WASHINGTON, DC; PHONE: 202-588-1471; FAX: 202-588-1472;
E-MAIL: witness@witnessforpeace.org;
WEB SITE: www.witnessforpeace.org

WOMEN'S INTERNATIONAL LEAGUE FOR PEACE AND FREEDOM

Works to achieve, through peaceful means, world disarmament, full rights for women, racial and economic justice, an end to all forms of violence, and to establish those political, social, and psychological conditions that can assure peace, freedom, and justice for all.

PHILADELPHIA, PA; PHONE: 215-563-7110; FAX: 215-563-5527;
E-MAIL: wilpf@wilpf.org; WEB SITE: www.wilpf.org

BOOKS, TAPES, VIDEOS

Getting to Peace: Transforming Conflict at Home, at Work, and in the World. William L. Ury. Viking Penguin, 1999.

Multi-Track Diplomacy: A Systems Approach to Peace. Louise Diamond and John McDonald. Kumarian Press, 1996.

"Newcomer's Guide to Track II Diplomacy." John McDonald. IMTD Occasional Paper Series, 1993. Available through IMTD, phone 202-466- 4605; Web site: www.imtd.org

WEB SITES

THE ALLIANCE FOR INTERNATIONAL CONFLICT
PREVENTION AND RESOLUTION (AICPR)

An alliance of 20-plus organizations doing conflict resolution and peacebuilding work internationally. Web site links to all member organizations.

www.aicpr.org

INTERACTION

A coalition of more than 165 nonprofit U.S.-based organizations doing international humanitarian work. Web site links to all member organizations.

www.interaction.org

UNESCO: DECADE OF THE CULTURE OF PEACE

Describes many activities associated with the UN Decade of Peace.

www.unesco.org

U.S. ASSOCIATION FOR THE
UN HIGH COMMISSIONER FOR REFUGEES

A click on this site provides a free donation for refugee relief.

www.peaceforall.com

Keywords to explore through your computer search engine: *world peace, peace on earth, global peace, relief and development, international peace, exchange programs, citizen diplomacy*

ELEVEN

PEACE & THE ENVIRONMENT

The Earth Is Alive

Who hears the rippling of rivers will not utterly despair of anything.
—HENRY DAVID THOREAU

Peace and the environment are intimately related. As the integrity of our natural systems erodes, resources necessary for survival become scarce. Land, water, minerals, and fossil fuels will be the battlegrounds of the twenty-first century. Already, communities everywhere are struggling with competing interests over short-term economic benefits versus the long-term sustainability of natural resources.

As we treat the Earth, so we treat each other. A culture of peace is a state of mind that values partnership and respect. We must approach the Earth in the same way. When we seek to dominate the natural environment, or take what we want without regard for the consequences or without respect for the living processes by which those resources are available, we destroy the peace of the whole sacred web of life, of which we are but a small part.

91   REALIZE THE INTERDEPENDENCE

Nature is one vast interconnected web of life. What happens in one place affects the whole web eventually. All life needs each other to thrive and survive.

Not only do we need each other, but we *are* each other. We drink water that came from the rivers; the minerals in the rocks are also in our bones; the sun warms us from the outside and through the life force in the food we eat. A true culture of peace requires that we live in ecological balance and harmony with all life.

• Honor "all your relations." Native American peoples acknowledge each and every being (whether two-legged or four-legged; the ones who fly, the ones who swim, and the ones who creep and crawl, the stone people and the plant people) as a relative. Greet the sun, a blade of grass, a frog, a bird as if it were your beloved cousin, aunt, or uncle.

• Sit by a tree. Think of all the ways your life depends on trees. Feel the sun on your face. Think of all the ways your life depends on the sun.

• Sift a handful of dirt through your fingers. Think of all the ways the soil depends on you. Dangle your feet into a stream or river. Think of all the ways the river depends on you.

• Name three things you do that support and enhance the environment around you. Name three things you do that harm the environment around you.

• Pick any one of your "relations" from the natural world—a bird, an insect, a plant. Learn what you can about that being: What is its habitat? Who are its natural enemies? Where does it get what it needs to survive? How has it been affected by human interaction?

92 TRACE THE NATURAL RESOURCES YOU DEPEND ON

We take so much for granted. We go through our days with food, shelter, clothing, transportation, and access to all sorts of activities, without ever taking the time to wonder how we are able to have what we have and do what we do.

Yet everything humans have and do can be traced back to the natural world, either directly or indirectly. When we pay attention to how this is so, we grow in appreciation and in a commitment to a good relationship with nature.

Ask yourself the following questions. Think carefully not only about what human activities are involved but also what natural life processes go on to make it possible for you to live as you do:

· How did the food get to your table? Take the food from any one meal and trace it back as far as you can, to see where it came from. Work backward from the table to the natural state.

· Where did the materials from which your house is constructed come from? Trace these materials in the same way as you did your food. What do you notice?

· How do you heat your home? How does that fuel come to you? Do the same exercise, following your warmth back to the elements.

· Where does your drinking water come from? How is your waste system (water, toilet, laundry) managed? Do the same tracing.

· What about the clothes you are wearing—what is their origin and journey from the natural state to your closet?

What do you learn from this exercise?

93 BECOME AN ENVIRONMENTAL CHAMPION AND STEWARD

Environmental problems are all around us: issues of water quality, air pollution, pesticides, dangerous waste products, mining and logging practices, dying oceans, climate changes, and many others.

These issues are too important to ignore. The choices we make now will affect our children many generations into the future. Each of us must commit to securing a sustainable future. We must act now to steward the precious resources of this Earth and to champion the cause of a healthy, balanced ecology.

• What are the local issues? Find out what your neighborhood, town, state, or region is struggling with. Find one issue that has particular interest for you.

• Get information. Inform yourself on this topic. Find out about the science involved; discover the different views being offered for solutions. Use this information to decide your own course of action.

• Get your whole family involved. We are in this together. Promote environmental awareness starting at home, by encouraging partners, children, parents, relatives, and friends to join you in addressing the concerns that affect us all.

• Think and act locally and globally. The immediate issues relate directly to your everyday life. The larger picture may seem more remote, but it is nonetheless important. Join a local action group, and also become a member of one of the large environmental groups dealing with similar issues at the level of national or international policy.

94   DO AN ENVIRONMENTAL INVENTORY OF YOUR HOME

Getting a good picture of your current relationship to environmental matters is the place to start your action.

ENVIRONMENTAL INVENTORY

Answer the following questions using this scale of frequency: 1—Never 2—Sometimes 3—Often 4—Always 5—Not applicable or not sure

In my home I (we):

_____ Recycle plastic

_____ Recycle newspapers

_____ Recycle junk mail

___ Recycle computer and office papers

___ Recycle cans

___ Recycle bottles

___ Make compost from kitchen and yard waste

___ Turn off electric lights and appliances when not in use

___ Turn off running water when not in immediate use

___ Refuse to buy articles wrapped unnecessarily in plastic

___ Use recycled paper for stationery

___ Use reusable cloth bags for grocery shopping

___ Use environmentally friendly household products

___ Test the water for contaminants periodically

___ Test the house for radon, asbestos, and other dangerous substances

___ Take care to store and dispose of hazardous products (paint, thinners, propane, kerosene, solvents) properly

Look at all the answers in the 1 or 2 range. This is the area where you can make the greatest change in your environmental habits.

95 CHANGE ONE THING IN YOUR ENVIRONMENTAL HABITS

Habits have a strong hold on our behavior. Something becomes a habit because it is repeated over and over again. To change a habit takes two things: commitment and practice.

Commitment comes when we make choices. Am I really willing to change? Do I say an unqualified "Yes" to this change? Will I follow through, even if I run into obstacles or if it's easier just to go back to my old way of doing things? Practice means doing the new behavior again and again as necessary until it is established as a familiar pattern.

• Review the results of your environmental inventory. Pick one habit from the inventory you seriously want to change. Make the commitment to change.

• Picture the new habit. Imagine what you would do differently if you were to make this change. Get information from others if you are not sure how to do it differently.

• Practice your new habit. Remind yourself gently when you forget. Recall your commitment to change. Is it still strong? Ask friends or family members to help you remember.

• Evaluate your success. After some time, retake the inventory to see if you have succeeded in changing your environmental habits.

96   GREEN UP YOUR NEIGHBORHOOD

Much can be done to make our own surroundings more environmentally sound. When we speak of "greening up" an area, we mean to make it more beautiful and alive. This means planting flowers, fruits, and vegetables; it means cleaning up trash; it means helping a paved area revert back to nature.

• Get creative with empty lots. If you find a piece of land being neglected or unused, join with others to find exciting ways to bring it back to nature (with permission of the owner, of course). Plant a wildflower garden; make a habitat for birds or small animals; make it into a mini-nature preserve; plant fruit trees or Christmas trees.

• Design a nature trail. Wherever you live, you can find some places of nature's beauty and wonder. Work with others to create a walking trail that goes through a natural area, with signposts and descriptive brochures to help people understand the marvel of nature they are witnessing.

• Plant flowers for beautification. Wherever there is a tiny piece of land or even room for a flower box—on street corners, on the green strip of lawn between street and sidewalk, beside the mailbox on a dusty country road—we can plant flowers for color and beauty, and to attract butterflies and birds.

• Do community trash clean-ups. Pick a street, a neighborhood, or a roadside, and go with a group of people and plenty of trash bags to clean up the mess.

• Include children in all these activities. Children can enjoy and learn from all green-up activities that environmental stewardship can be fun and is the natural responsibility of everyone in the community.

97 GROW FOOD

Growing food requires intimate participation in the processes of life and in the cycles of nature. All the elements come together to produce food. The Earth, sun, rain, and fresh air all are needed by the seeds to grow to their greatest potential.

Even in the largest cities, we can connect in some way with the life cycle by raising our own food and feeding our friends. When we plant, tend, harvest, and eat this food, we remember that we too are part of this sacred chain of life.

• Plant windowsill herbs. Parsley, oregano, thyme, dill, basil, and other cooking herbs do well in small pots in sunny windows.

• Plant container gardens on roofs or patios. Big buckets, pots, or planting boxes are great for places where the earth is covered with concrete or brick or where there is little space for a garden.

• Join community gardens. Each person or family might have their own garden within a larger plot of land, or people might work together on a single garden. If there are no community gardens in your area, start one.

• Join a gardening co-op. Look for or start a garden where one person tends the crop while members provide the cash necessary for the labor and equipment, and then are entitled to a share of the produce.

• Support organic gardening. Whether you get your food from your own backyard, a garden co-op, a local farmer, or the grocery store, insist on food raised organically—without the use of harmful fertilizers, pesticides, hormones, and other chemicals.

• Barter for produce. If you cannot grow your own food but know others who do, offer to barter. Give something you have or can do in exchange for the produce you want. This honors the cycle of reciprocity.

98   GROW BEAUTY

Beauty, like peace, is our soul's birthright. We nourish ourselves in the deepest way when we make and share beauty. Beauty provides inspiration as well as sanctuary. It helps us attune to that place of deep inner peace at our core. It encourages balance and serenity.

When beauty is connected to nature and to nature's cycles of life, it is even more compelling. Then we are reminded of our place in the universe and of the natural harmony of all creation.

• Add color to your surroundings. Inside your home and outside, have flowers that are colorful, vibrant, and cheerful.

• Turn eyesores into places of special beauty. Choose an over-grown piece of land, a trash heap, a barren strip of asphalt, or a neglected or abused piece of city property. Gather the resources—human, financial, technical—to turn it into a place of beauty—perhaps a park, a playground, or a sculpture garden.

• Build sanctuaries and peace gardens. The smallest area, beauti-fully planted and designed, can be designated as a peace garden, a sanctuary from the hustle and bustle of everyday life.

• Combine natural beauty with human art. Add murals, sculpture, graphic designs, music, and poetry to gardens, parks, and woods.

• Support public use of natural areas. Help keep the parks clean and accessible. Encourage the creation of nature trails and bike and walking paths. Insist on public access to waterfront property and beaches. Support city, state, and national parks and monu-ments. Work to ensure that these areas stay beautiful as well as available.

99   GIVE THANKS

Being grateful goes naturally with feeling joy and peace. Our grati-tude for life itself—for the processes of nature that allow us to be present in this body, on this Earth—is a way of connecting with the web of creation.

Gratitude is also a way of giving something back. Nature gives to us all the time, without judging our worthiness. If we just take and never give back, it's like only breathing in and never breathing out.

Saying "Thank you" is how we return a blessing for the blessings we receive every day. It is how we stay in balance.

· Adopt an attitude of gratitude. Let gratefulness be how you are and move in the world. See everything—especially every part of the natural world—as the gift that it is.

· Practice thankfulness rituals. For each meal, for each glass or water, for all that the Earth provides, develop personal and family rituals to show your gratitude.

· Make offerings. Give something back to the Earth. Offer prayers to the land where the land is especially bountiful or where it is especially hurt. Go to a river and place a flower on the current to carry your thankfulness downstream.

· Be aware of the bounty. Life is lavish with its gifts. Nature's abundance sustains you a thousand ways every day. Take a moment to recognize the feast that is spread before you through the generosity of Earth and sky.

· Provide for others. Show gratitude for all you receive by sharing generously with others, especially those who may not have all that you do. Pass along the bounty of nature's gifts to those who are without access to healthy and abundant food, clean water, or a safe and warm home.

REVIEW

Practice the Four Principles of Peace and the Environment

COMMUNITY
Remember your core connection to the natural
world, and be an environmental champion and steward.

COOPERATION
Work with others to make gardens,
parks, and places of natural beauty.

NONVIOLENCE
Open your heart in gratitude for nature's endless gifts.

WITNESS
Be a living model of environmental awareness.

AN ENVIRONMENTAL SUCCESS STORY

When business interests collide with environmental and quality of life concerns, sparks can fly. How communities deal with such competing interests can determine whether there is bitterness and enmity or peaceful resolution and cooperation. The woman who tells this story was helpful in turning this potential conflict into a community success story.

A few years ago, a small family-owned granite company wanted to expand a quarry in a rural residential area. The local residents were alarmed and demanded that state officials stop the project at all costs. Tensions on both sides were very high.

I was the official they turned to. Flush with having just completed a basic mediation course, I asked the residents if they had talked with the quarry owners. No, they had not, and they would not, as they were convinced that no one would listen. I suggested that everyone sit down together and discuss the issues.

After a rocky beginning (participants began by screaming obscenities at each other), the mediation went very well. The quarry operators listened respectfully to the concerns of the neighbors, and the neighbors slowly began to have a bit of trust in the father-and-son-run company. As tensions eased, the discussion shifted from angry accusations to collaborative problem solving:

"What can we do to make sure that trucks leaving the quarry are driven safely on neighborhood roads?"

"How can blasting be scheduled so as to minimize noise impacts on neighbors?" (The final agreement took into account the nap schedule of a two-year-old who lived nearby.)

"Where can berms be placed to absorb noise?"

At the end of the second mediation session, the participants had an agreement among themselves that made state involvement unneccessary. As I was leaving, I heard several people talking about having a picnic in a few months to get to know each other better and to work out any problems that developed.

RESOURCE GUIDE

Check within your local community for environmental awareness or action programs, for nature walks, community gardens, and green-up events. Here are some suggestions:

PROGRAMS AND ORGANIZATIONS

THE NATURAL STEP

A nonprofit environmental organization working to build an ecologically and economically sustainable society. Offers a framework that is based in science and serves as a compass for organizations and individuals working to redesign their activities to become more sustainable.

SAN FRANCISCO, CA; PHONE: 415-561-3344; FAX: 415-561-3345:
E-MAIL: tns@naturalstep.org; WEB SITE: www.naturalstep.org

RESOLVE

Specializes in building consensus on environmental, health, sustainable communities, and other public policy issues. Provides mediation, facilitation, research, training, and coaching for effective collaboration and partnership efforts.

WASHINGTON, DC; PHONE: 202-944-2300;
E-MAIL: gbingham@resolv.org; WEB SITE: www.resolv.org

SUSTAINABILITY INSTITUTE

A think/do tank dedicated to sustainable resource use, sustainable economy, and sustainable community. Provides information, analysis, and practical demonstrations that can foster transitions to sustainable systems.

HARTLAND FOUR CORNERS, VT; PHONE: 802-436-2333;
E-MAIL: hhamilton@centerss.org; WEB SITE: www.sustainer.org

BOOKS, TAPES, VIDEOS

The Consumer's Guide to Effective Environmental Choices: Practical Advice from the Union of Concerned Scientists. Michael Brower and Warren Leon. Three Rivers Press, 1999.

Deep Ecology for the Twenty-First Century. George Sessions, ed. Shambhala, 1994.

Dharma Rain: Sources of Buddhist Environmentalism. Kenneth Kraft, and Stephanie Kaza, ed. Shambhala, 2000.

Earth in Balance: Ecology of the Human Spirit. Al Gore. Plume, 1993.

Ecology of Hope: Communities Collaborate for Sustainability. Ted Bernard and Jora Young. Adapted by Wes Jackson. New Society Publishers, 1996.

Silent Spring. Rachel Carson. Houghton Mifflin Co., 1993.

WEB SITES

ECONET
Articles, discussions, action alerts, eco news.
www.igc.org/igc/gateway/enindex.html

GREEN PAGES
Directory of thousands of socially and environmentally responsible businesses, products and services.
www.coopamerica.org/gp

Keywords to explore through your computer search engine: *ecology, environmental action, environmental sustainability, environment*

TWELVE

PEACE & SPIRIT
Shining the Light of Peace

This little light of mine,
I'm gonna let it shine. . . .
—A TRADITIONAL GOSPEL SONG

T he journey for peace—inner peace and peace on Earth—is ultimately a spiritual journey. Our souls long for peace. Our spirit
hungers to come home to its source, where Peace and Love
reside unconditionally. When we remember our natural self, we swim
in this essence. Thus, this final chapter completes the circle begun in
the first chapter, on finding true inner peace.

The major religions of the world hold peace as a central goal
and core value. Yet we do not have to be religious in the conventional
sense to experience the spiritual dimension of peace. We need only
connect with our true nature and know that we are part of something
larger. We need only trust that whatever that greater whole (being,

power, mystery, energy, God, divine essence) is, peace is at its sacred center—and so are we.

100 FIND YOUR PLACE IN THE UNIVERSE

The universe is vast and mysterious beyond imagining. The age-old question of "Who am I?" in relation to that great mystery continues to capture our attention. This is not a question for which we have definitive answers. Asking it periodically gives us the chance to unfold more and more of who we really are.

• Sit quietly with a friend or with pen and paper. Ask yourself, "Who am I?" or have your friend ask, "Who are you?" Answer. Ask the same question again. Give a different answer, whatever comes into your mind.

• Keep asking and answering that same question, pushing past your level of discomfort, even when you think there are no more answers to give. There are no right and wrong answers, just increasing levels of awareness.

• Stand outside on a starry night, somewhere where you have a good view of the night sky. Ask repeatedly, "Who am I?" Again, listen for the many answers that come.

• Hold a baby. Peer into the center of a beautiful flower. Put on the most beautiful music you know and listen (with earphones, if possible). Stand at the ocean's edge. Ask again, "Who am I?" Listen for what comes back.

101 HEAL OLD WOUNDS WITH GOD AND RELIGION

Many people have trouble moving forward in their spiritual life because of unhealed wounds from the past. Perhaps the religion in which we grew up felt punitive or empty. Perhaps we suffered or witnessed a great tragedy, and wondered how any Divine Being could allow such evil or anguish. Or we may have felt betrayed by a trusted religious figure.

When we carry these old scars in our mindstream, it is difficult to be at peace with ourselves and our world, for our spiritual peace is at the heart of all our relationships. The split from Spirit makes honoring the Four Principles of Peace more of a task than a joy.

- Sit quietly, alone or with a trusted friend. Tell the story of your spiritual journey to date.

- Make note of the places in the story where you still have some negative emotional charge or reaction. Identify the wounds still to be healed.

- If you have moved away from your original religion, consider why that was. You may want to go back to the mosque, temple, shrine, sacred fire, church, or synagogue (either the exact one you used to attend or one like it) to see how it feels in the present time. Sing the songs or chants; practice the rituals. What do you notice?

- If you didn't have a religious upbringing or have not pursued any religious study or experience, ask yourself why. Try attending a variety of places of worship, or reading spiritually oriented books, to see what you notice.

- Find the right medicine to help mend whatever has been damaged. Is there someone you need to express your feelings to? Something you need to let go of? Someone to forgive (including yourself, or even God)? Something you need to talk about in a safe space?

- Take one step toward healing this most central of all relationships, trusting that further steps will follow in the right time if that is your desire.

102   PRAY FOR PEACE; MEDITATE FOR PEACEFULNESS

Some say that prayer is speaking to God (or whatever name you give to that great spiritual force), and that meditation is listening to God. Both prayer and meditation come in many forms. Prayer can be a statement of gratitude, a petition or request, a wish, the sending forth of a specific positive thought—through attunement to a higher source or your higher self, however you understand that.

Meditation might involve conscious breathing, watching and releasing thoughts that arise, repetition of a word or sound, focus on an object or image, or just resting in the great emptiness.

Many studies have shown the positive effects of both prayer and meditation on the body and the mind. Something definitely happens in our energy field and in the fields of those around us, when we pray and meditate. If we pray and meditate for peace, even over long distances, we literally give peace power.

• Find a prayer for peace in some scripture, sacred, or inspirational text. Read it to yourself, read it aloud, memorize it. Pray it with all your heart.

• Make up a prayer for peace. Pray it with all your soul.

• Send out that prayer for peace to the people you'd like it to benefit. Send it with all your might. See it fulfilled—for instance, see the people suffering from war able to stop the fighting and rebuild sane and trusting relationships.

• Find or create a song that carries a spiritual message of peace meaningful to you. Sing it with all your soul.

• Learn a meditation technique that works for you. Practice it regularly. Let it center you home to the place of inner peace.

103   FIND AN INSPIRATIONAL ROLE MODEL

A spiritual role model is someone—living or dead or even imaginary—who represents for you the highest spiritual ideal. This person or being represents the qualities you would like to attain and inspires you to reach for them.

This role model is a doorway onto your spiritual path, and a guide and friend along the way. It both pushes you to stretch beyond your presumed limits and invites you into new and exciting sacred territory.

• Identify a person or a being who especially inspires you, touches your soul.

Find a picture of this great one. Or draw one that shows how you think they might look.

• Put the picture somewhere where you will see it every day. Look at the picture as if you were looking into the mirror. See yourself reflected in the eyes of this being. Try on their good qualities, as if they were your own.

• Read whatever words may have been written by or about this person. Write words you think they might write if they could.

• Talk to your friends and family about this spiritual ideal and what it means to you.

104   WATER THE SEEDS OF PEACE IN EVERYTHING AND EVERYONE

In every situation, no matter how conflictual, the seeds of peace exist. In every person, no matter how distressed, the seeds of peace exist. These seeds exist because we exist; they are part of us from birth, part of our spiritual DNA patterning. Peace is always possible, because it is encoded within us as our sacred birthright.

Seeds, like acorns, carry the imprint of their own maturity. The seed is the potential; it is programmed for success. Sometimes the seed needs a little help in order to grow. Seeds especially need careful watering.

• Practice looking at every person you meet as if they were the living embodiment of Peace. Try it with yourself as well.

• When someone is breaking the peace, hold the thought that the seeds of peace they have temporarily forgotten might be remembered. Actively water those seeds by addressing that potential in the person rather than reacting to the immediate behavior.

• In any conflict situation you are involved in, or a witness to, give your attention to the possibility for peace. Never let go of that awareness, no matter what the circumstances might seem like. In fact, the worse the circumstances appear, the stronger you need to be calling out that potential. Pray that this potential might be realized.

• If the conflict seems impossible to resolve, pray for the miracle of peace. Pray for peace to blossom, even if you cannot find the formula for its flowering.

105   HONOR THE SPIRIT OF PEACE IN ACTION

This inner pattern for peace is not an inert possibility; it is a living presence that we can call the Spirit of Peace. The Spirit of Peace longs to be activated, set in motion, so that peace itself can be a force for good in our relationships and in the world. In this way, Spirit lives through us, and life is peace in action.

When we see the Spirit of Peace in action we need to honor it, so it will grow. To become part of our everyday culture, peacebuilding activities need to be known, seen, and heard about. We need a promotion campaign for peace.

• When anyone does something—no matter how small—to increase peace in any aspect of life, applaud them. Let them know how grateful you are for their courage and example.

• When you see a success story for peace, spread the word about it. Write it up for your local newspaper; tell your friends; call it in to a radio talk show.

• Collect success stories and put them on the Internet. E-mail them to your friends.

• When your own efforts in any of the activities listed in this book bear fruit, let people know. Don't be shy; practice shameless acts of self-promotion for peace.

• Get together with others and plan a mini-advertising campaign to inform people about one aspect of peacebuilding or non-violent conflict resolution.

• Encourage your workplace, place of worship, or community organization to host an awards dinner to honor the most outstanding peacebuilders in your group.

106   LOVE LIFE AND ALL WHO LIVE

Peace, life, and love are intertwined in our being. To be fully alive is to know peace; to love peace is to love life; to live peace is to live love. The Spirit of Peace is also the Spirit of Love and the Spirit of Life. Spirit is one.

To know and express our love for peace, we express our love for all who share this planet with us, for all who live, for all our relatives. In respecting life, we honor that potential for peace that is within us all. In respecting the whole family of life, we honor the sacred circle of all that is.

• Hug a tree; bless a star; say "Thank you" to a butterfly; cherish a worm; caress a leaf; blow a kiss to a bumblebee; tickle the grass; pat a cat. Treat all life as your favorite relative.

• If there is any creature that you are afraid of or that repulses you, find something to like about them. Spend one hour getting to know all you can about them. Pretend that this creature is your best friend.

• When you wake up in the morning, offer a prayer of gratitude that you are alive. Fill your lungs with fresh air, and feel the fullness of life.

• When you go to sleep at night, list the highlights of your day. What were the best moments? What can you celebrate?

• Make an offering of your joy. Whenever something happens during the day that brings you happiness, important life lessons, or a moment of peace, dedicate the benefit of it to others. Make a simple prayer that whatever good you are experiencing might ripple out from you and bring the same good to others.

107   LIGHT UP THE WORLD

Many faith traditions speak of Spirit as Light. Light is the essence of our spiritual nature. The Bible says, "Don't hide your light under a bushel." When we shine the light of peace, we are dressing the Spirit of Peace in all its radiant glory.

The eternal light, the lamp, the torch, the flame, the candle—these are archetypal metaphors, across cultures and throughout time. They signify a light that is sacred, holy, inspiring, inviting. When peace is our lamp, people can find their way through any darkness.

• Know yourself as light. You are a being of light. Your unique flame of life burns bright and strong. You are part of a larger fire, the inner light that ignites us all from the same source.

• Imagine that your body is full of stars. You are shining from the inside out. Feel this as the light of peace. Turn up the volume, and send it out. Radiate peace.

• Pretend you are a lighthouse. Flash that beacon of light in all directions, so that those who are lost in the violent seas might find their way safely home to peace. Direct the beam of light especially to those places in your nation or around the world where people are suffering the anguish of war.

• Become, for a moment, like the Statue of Liberty. Hold up the torch, the light of peace, that the oppressed of the world can have hope that peace is possible.

• Play with other metaphors for light: flashlight, candle, campfire, light bulb, starlight, sunlight. Think of new ones. Draw them, be them, act them out. However you can experience yourself as light is useful in reminding you that you can, through conscious choice, light up the world and your unique corner of it.

108 LAUGH A LOT

When we know ourselves as light, as Spirit, as one with all life, we feel boundless joy. Joy and its physical expression, laughter, are the natural language of the Spirit of Peace.

Medical practitioners know that laughter has great healing power during times of sickness. We even have a saying, "Laughter is the best medicine." We can get to the joy through laughter, or to the laughter through joy. It doesn't matter. What does matter is that we celebrate the Spirit of Peace with joy.

• Play the laughing game. Several people lie down, each with their head on someone's belly. One person starts laughing. Soon all the bellies are bouncing with laughter, and no one can stop!

• Be silly. Don't worry what you look like or what people will say. Do something totally unusual, ridiculous, and laughable. Make a fool of yourself.

• Go to the video store and take out five comedies you have never seen. Tell your friends about the three best ones.

- Pick a favorite comedian and watch, read, or listen to much of their work. Become a Lucy expert, a Dave Barry fan, or a *Saturday Night Live* aficionado.

- Enroll in clown school.

- Tell jokes. When you hear a funny joke, write it down and practice telling it to your family. Or get a joke book and try some.

- Be like a child. No matter how old you are, you can be playful. Tease, hop, skip rope, imagine, wonder, focus completely and earnestly on one small thing, be full of awe.

- Remember three of the most joyous moments in your life. Tell someone about them, savoring every bit of the memory.

- Be at peace with the joy of life.

REVIEW

Practice the Four Principles of the Spirit of Peace

COMMUNITY
Cherish all that lives.

COOPERATION
Work with the Spirit of Peace in action; make it real.

NONVIOLENCE
Acknowledge the seeds for peace in all people and all situations.

WITNESS
Practice the living presence of peace;
shine your light as a beacon of hope.

HEALING THE HOLY WOUND

How easy it is to get caught in day-to-day life in the material realm and forget our spiritual nature! Sometimes, if we look deeply, we might actually discover a moment when we made a choice to forget. Here is a story of blessed remembrance, when one man's temporal pain turned inside out to reveal a long-hidden sense of wholeness and joy.

On the surface, my life seemed great. I had a wonderful family, an exciting job, a lovely home. Yet from time to time I would experience waves of anguish and despair.

One day, when I felt particularly bad, I went for a walk on the beach. It was an early winter day, and I had the beach to myself. I started talking out loud, to whom I wasn't sure. I complained bitterly about the unexplainable hole in my life. Why wasn't I satisfied? What else did I need?

When I wore myself out with moaning and groaning, I looked around me, noticing the beach and its beauty in what seemed like a new way. There was a strange shimmering quality of light on the curling tops of the waves. A thought, like a voice, came into my mind: "Here I am," it said. "Here who is?" I asked. "Here I am. Here, I am," repeated the thought.

Suddenly a memory came—the moment I decided not to go to church anymore because I couldn't stand the hypocrisy of the religion-on-Sunday-only crowd. I saw how I had cut spirituality out of my life with that decision. Now I knew what had been missing. I looked around and found in that instant a new church, the church of here, where I am, where my heart is open and my senses alive, where the vast forces of life work mysteriously but surely, and I am part of it all.

I found a beautiful shell on the beach. I stood for a moment with it in my hand and waited for a prayer. The prayer that came was gratitude, pure and simple, for the joy of life. I gave the shell back to the water, from whence it came.

RESOURCE GUIDE

Check within your local community for special prayer services for peace, for programs of meditation instruction, for spiritual or religious activities related to peace. Here are some suggestions:

PROGRAMS AND ORGANIZATIONS

AMERICAN FRIENDS SERVICE COMMITTEE

Quaker organization that includes people of all faiths who are committed to social justice, peace, and humanitarian service. Focuses on issues related to economic justice, peacebuilding, demilitarization, social justice, and youth, in the United States and around the world.

PHILADELPHIA, PA; PHONE: 215-241-7000; FAX: 215-241-7275;
E-MAIL: afscinfo@asfc.org; WEB SITE: www.afsc.org

MENNONITE CENTRAL COMMITTEE

A relief, service, community development and peace agency of the North American Mennonite and Brethren in Christ churches. The Mennonite Conciliation Service (MCS) is a network of individuals committed to transforming conflict. Teaches effective conflict resolution skills and promotes positive attitudes toward conflict.

AKRON, PA; PHONE: 717-859-1151;
E-MAIL: mccwash@mcc.org; WEB SITE: mcc@mcc.org

SUNRAY MEDITATION SOCIETY

An international spiritual society dedicated to planetary peace. Home fire of the Green Mountain Aniyunwiwa (Cherokee) and a Tibetan Buddhist Dharma center of the Nyingma and Drikung Kagyu schools, Sunray offers practical and skillful methods for realizing peace, compassion, and right relationship with Earth and all relations. Ongoing programs of education, service, and spiritual training.

BRISTOL, VT; PHONE: 802-453-4610;
E-MAIL: sunray@sover.net; WEB SITE: www.sunray.org

UNITED RELIGIONS INITIATIVE

A growing global community dedicated to building cultures of peace and justice to serve a better future for the Earth Community. People around the globe have joined together, celebrating the uniqueness of their traditions, to explore how interfaith cooperation can make a positive difference in their local communities.

SAN FRANCISCO, CA; PHONE: 415-561-2300; FAX: 415-561-2313; E-MAIL: office@uri.org; WEB SITE: www.united-religions.org

BOOKS, TAPES, VIDEOS

Attitudes of Gratitude: How to Give and Receive Joy Every Day of Your Life. Mary Jane Ryan. Conari Press, 1999.

Being Peace. Thich Nhat Hanh. Parallax Press, 1988.

Compassion in Action: Setting Out on the Path of Service. Ram Dass. Crown Publishing Group, 1992.

The Courage for Peace: Daring to Create Harmony in Ourselves and the World. Louise Diamond. Conari Press, 1999.

Praying Peace. James Twyman, Gregg Braden, and Doreen Virtue, Findhorn Press, 2000. Available from Source Books, P.O. Box 292231, Nashville, TN 37229-2231; phone: 800-637-5222.

Seeking Peace: Notes and Conversations Along the Way. Johann Christoph Arnold. Dutton/Plume, 2000.

Voices of Our Ancestors: Cherokee Teachings from the Wisdom Fire. Dhyani Ywahoo. Shambhala, 1987.

WEB SITES

AMERICAN FRIENDS SERVICE COMMITTEE

Online magazine, *Peacework,* offering resources and articles from AFSC.

ww.afsc.org/peacewrk.html

BELIEFNET

The largest and most acclaimed multifaith spirituality website.

www.beliefnet.com

Council for a Parliament of the World's Religions
www.cpwr.org

EMISSARY OF LIGHT
Offers books, music, newsletter, workshop information, and message board relating to the work of Jimmy Twyman, Peace Troubadour.
www.emissaryoflight.com

RELIGIOUS PEACE FELLOWSHIPS
Numerous faith-based associations committed to peace. Affiliated with the Fellowship of Reconciliation. Includes:

The Baptist Peace Fellowship
www.bpfna.org

The Buddhist Peace Fellowship
www.bpf.org

The Episcopal Peace Fellowship
www.episcopalpeacefellowship.org

The Jewish Peace Fellowship
www.jewishpeacefellowship.org

The Muslim Peace Fellowship
www.mpfweb.org

The Orthodox Peace Fellowship
www.incommunion.org

Keywords to explore through your computer search engine: *spiritual peace, religion and peace*

EPILOGUE
Join the Peace Revolution

I am only one; but still I am one.
I cannot do everything, but still I can do something.
I will not refuse to do something I can do.
—HELEN KELLER

IMAGINE, REVISITED

Now that you have read this book, can you imagine a world where people do the things suggested here as a matter of course? Can you see, feel, and sense how our social discourse and popular culture would be different?

Having read this book, now imagine a world where:

· People touch their place of inner peace at will.

· Our family life is grounded in a commitment to win-win solutions.

· Our children grow up learning to solve their problems non-violently and cooperatively.

- At work we honor diversity and teamwork, and promote peace in and through our jobs.

- We naturally practice civil discourse and respectful dialogue in our communities, seeking common ground and consensus on controversial issues.

- We truly honor the diversity of our human family and build bridges of understanding instead of walls of separation.

- We routinely apologize, forgive, and make amends to heal where we have hurt and been hurt.

- Social and economic justice and human rights are honored through right action and just institutional structures throughout society.

- Nonviolence replaces violence as a core value of our culture.

- World peace is the work of all the people.

- We take our role as stewards and champions of the environment seriously.

- We understand life as the Spirit of Peace in action.

This world can become a reality through the thought, word, and deed of each and every person reading this book. You CAN make a difference. You CAN make the peace revolution come alive. Acting together, we CAN build a strong and viable culture of peace to replace the culture of violence now prevalent in our society.

USING THIS BOOK AS A BLUEPRINT FOR ACTION

In the Introduction, we spoke about the peace revolution as a massive shift in consciousness that will allow us to replace the prevailing culture of violence with a new culture of peace. We spoke about the UN Decade of the Culture of Peace as an opportunity to change the way we live together on this planet. We spoke about a revolutionary moment, when, through our collective thought and action, we can actually bring about a new set of conditions for how our society functions.

To build any structure, we need a blueprint. The blueprint takes the intention and the ideas for structure and translates them into a visible plan for action. It shows us not only how things will look at the end, but how to reach that end, step by step. It also shows us the different parts in relation to each other.

Celebrate Peace is meant to be a blueprint for building a revolutionary social structure, one founded in the Four Principles of Peace. It is meant as a guide to action. Taken individually and together, the 108 practical suggestions offered here can, if enough people will adopt them, be the bricks and mortar of the peace revolution.

One hundred and eight activities are only a small fraction of what is possible to build a new culture of peace. What is possible is whatever we set our minds to.

The first question, then, is, Will I join the peace revolution? Will I make a commitment to building a culture of peace through my life's actions? If the answer is "Yes," read on. If the answer is "I'm not sure," read on. If the answer is "No," read on anyway. Perhaps you will change your mind.

The second question is, What can I do to promote the peace revolution? The answer to that question is limited only by your own imagination and willingness to try new things.

Certainly, *Celebrate Peace* gives you a good place to start.

• Read the book, using the section on page xiii, "A Reader's Guide to *Celebrate Peace*" for tips on how to get the most out of your experience with it.

• Do one thing suggested in this book; do one thing from each chapter of the book.

• Give the book to a friend or family member, to a colleague, or a stranger; tell people how this book has affected your life.

• Start a study group to discuss this book. Do some of the activities together. Discuss the results. Explore together what you are learning. Help start other study groups. Create a network of study groups, all using *Celebrate Peace* as the foundation for action and learning.

• Think of—and do—other activities, not mentioned in the book, that help build a culture of peace. Let's make the list grow from 108 to 1,008; to 10,008; to 100,008, and beyond.

• Introduce *Celebrate Peace* to your local school system. Work with teachers, parents, principals, school boards, and students to find creative ways to use this book as part of the educational process. Arrange to have every high school graduate (or middle school graduate, or college graduate) in your town (or state) receive a copy of *Celebrate Peace* along with their diploma.

• Plan special public events to share *Celebrate Peace* and to promote some of the ideas suggested in it. Host a community picnic where cooperative games for peace are played. Encourage one store in the mall to do a day-long promotion, giving *Celebrate Peace* to every customer who walks in the door. Organize a teach-in at the park. Get famous people involved. Call a press conference. Develop a public relations campaign. Lobby your local libraries and bookstores to use *Celebrate Peace* as the focal point of a new section dedicated exclusively to books on peace. The list could go on and on. Whatever you do, put the information on our website to help others think of good ideas for their community.

• Give *Celebrate Peace* as a Gift of Peace to family, friends, and colleagues as a way to change the world, one 'peace' at a time. see the back cover for more information.

In other words, the possibilities are endless for using *Celebrate Peace* as a vehicle for raising consciousness about the peace revolution. The peace revolution is not just a crazy ideal. It already exists, in its infancy. Only through committed action in our personal and public lives will the peace revolution flourish, changing the world as we know it. Only then will our children have a real chance to live, truly, "the peace that passeth understanding."

What are we waiting for? Let's get creative. Let's get excited. Let's get going!

A Teacher's Guide to *Celebrate Peace*

Obviously, how *Celebrate Peace* can be incorporated into a school curriculum will vary widely depending on grade level, local interests, and other factors. You can be endlessly creative in how you use the book. However, here are seven possible approaches for teachers:

1 Consider your overall curriculum for the year. Find sections of *Celebrate Peace* that correspond with the material you will be covering. Include those sections when the right time comes, as a supplement to your study plan.

2 Each week during the school year, set aside a thirty-minute period to cover one item from *Celebrate Peace*. Let the students take responsibility for selecting the topic, maybe even for deciding how the class will deal with the material. Let this be the highlight of the week, something for the students to look forward to. Encourage them to make it particularly exciting, interactive, and fun.

3 Pick one of the twelve chapters, or one of the 108 practical tips, and design a whole unit of study around it. Weave in other instructional elements: creative writing, group discussion, skits, poetry, puzzles, drawing, cooperative games.

4 Let students, working individually or in small groups, pick one of the 108 practical tips and do a research project on it, making a presentation to the rest of the class on their results. The research can use the Resource Guides provided in the book or might explore resources in your local community. Or it might be an opportunity to use the Internet to gather information.

5 Let the students work in small groups to do media projects based on any of the 108 practical tips, using print journalism, audio or radio technology, video, multimedia, computer software.

6 Ask each student to pick one of the 108 practical tips and use it as a basis to do a ten-hour community service project.

7 Ask the class to write a new chapter of *Celebrate Peace* specifically geared toward kids their own age. Send the results to our website: *www.thepeacecompany.com.* In fact, send the results of all of your activities to the website, so that others can learn from your experiences.

In addition to these classroom suggestions, you might think of interesting assembly programs, ways to include parents, and avenues for getting students to interact with their larger communities.

A Study Group Guide
to *Celebrate Peace*

Perhaps you already belong to a study group of some kind, like a peace committee at your place of worship, a current affairs discussion group, or a book club. If not, you can create one easily enough by simply declaring that you are starting a study group to explore the ideas raised in *Celebrate Peace*. Invite people you know who might be interested. The size of the group is not important (though too large a group might be cumbersome). You can meet weekly, monthly, or for an intensive weekend.

While you will find all kinds of ways to use this book on your own, here are a few simple suggestions for a group:

1 Pick a chapter a week for 12 weeks. Discuss it together. Each member of the group pick one item from the chapter, do the activity before the meeting, and come prepared to talk about the results and to lead the group in doing it.

2 Pick a single topic and stay with it over time until you have exhausted the conversation.

3 Pick a single item among the 108 (a different one each meeting). First, read it together and make sure you all understand what it says. Discuss the meaning it carries for you. Then, do some of the suggested activities together. Talk about what you learned. What further

questions did this raise for you? What might be some next steps?

4 Pick one item from among the 108 and make a group project out of it. Plan an activity that you can do together or that you can take out to the larger community.

5 Pick one of the self-inventories in the book and take the test during your meeting, and discuss the results with each other.

6 Work together to come up with at least three new practical tips for each of the 12 chapters. Send your results to The Peace Company (email: info@thepeacecompany.com), so others might benefit from your creative thinking.

A Web User's Guide to *Celebrate Peace*

Celebrate Peace is meant to be used by individuals, and also to be a collective and interactive experience. It is meant to be a catalyst for action on a large scale. The Internet can be an especially effective tool for moving this peace revolution to that larger dimension, because it is all about networks. Leveraging existing networks—and forming new ones—is exactly how a peace revolution will succeed.

Here are seven suggestions for people who are at least mildly literate in the Internet for using *Celebrate Peace* to spread the culture of peace.

1 Check out the website addresses given in the Resource Guide. Use one to get you to others; follow the path of interest that unfolds from one site to the next. Interact on those sites, and in doing so, mention *Celebrate Peace* so that its message spreads through a vast network.

2 As you find new websites of interest to the growing *Celebrate Peace* community of readers, send that information back to The Peace Company (email: *info@thepeacecompany.com*).

3 Do a book review of *Celebrate Peace.* Write a few paragraphs about its impact on you, and send that over your personal e-mail network to friends and family.

4 Make The Peace Company website a regular stop on your Internet journeys. Visit it frequently to read the latest news on the progress of the peace revolution.

5 Use The Peace Company website as a way to communicate with others. Send your ideas, your success stories, your challenges, and your experiences with *Celebrate Peace* to us, so we might share them with others (email: info@thepeacecompany.com).

6 Do web-based research on topics suggested by *Celebrate Peace*.

7 Think of *Celebrate Peace* website as a giant hub, or wheel, around which the peace revolution spins. It is both a source and a receptacle for information, communication, education, networking, and dialogue. Those who are especially skilled in Internet use can help the rest of us by finding unusual, creative, and exciting new ways to use both *Celebrate Peace* and its website as effective tools in making peace the way we live.

Acknowledgments

The Peace Book is a river fed by many streams.

MY OWN JOURNEY ON THE PEACE PATH

My personal journey—and therefore every thought and word in this book—has been assisted, guided, supported, and empowered by many very special people. I am so deeply grateful to those whose generosity has made my path, and this book, possible:

• The Venerable Dhyani Ywahoo, my spiritual teacher and friend, for her rich and ancient wisdom that is like the breath of inspiration, infusing every page of *The Peace Book;* and for her love;

• Ambassador John McDonald, my partner and mentor in the realm of international peacebuilding, for his wealth of practical expertise—gathered over decades of experience all around the world; for his patience and understanding in the laboratory of our partnership; and for his unwavering commitment to peace;

• Richard Moon and Chris Thorsen, for helping me understand and integrate the art of Aikido as the art of peacebuilding, and for their lasting friendship;

• The thousands of colleagues and fellow peacebuilders around the world, in places like Cyprus, Bosnia, India, Pakistan, Kenya, Israel, Palestine, Tanzania, Liberia, Sri Lanka, and elsewhere, for showing me the real blueprint for peace.

SPECIAL THANKS TO . . .

Ruth Hoffman was the very first to support *The Peace Book,* and her generous sponsorship provided the means to complete the book and get it through the publishing process. Ruth has a longtime commitment to peace and justice, which she consistently demonstrates through her community involvement and by the way she lives her life. Her special interests include hospice, Jungian psychology, and family. Ruth lives in New England, where she is a pillar of love and light to her children, grandchildren, and many, many friends.

Two friends who wish to remain anonymous have also provided generous support for *The Peace Book.* Their assistance made possible the many activities involved in bringing the project to fruition. They have a deep commitment to the well-being of the planet and all its inhabitants, with a particular interest in peace, healing, sacred space, and the health of our earth and ocean environments. They are well-known for the quality of love they express in their lives.

The Peace Book PROJECT

I could not possibly have undertaken this project alone. Along the way, a few people have offered support, encouragement, and practical help in various forms, always when it was just needed. I am so grateful to them:

• Denise Kaufman, for being the first to listen to this idea, and for letting me know I wasn't crazy;

• Maura Gannon Swift, Louise Piche, Diane Rooney, and Graeme Marsh, for believing in *The Peace Book;* for believing in the peace revolution; for believing in me; and for working hard to make it happen;

• Marji Greenhut, for putting the idea forward in places where it could make a difference; and for being a good friend along the shoreline of life;

- Judy Filner, Shannon Anton, and Paula Green for their untiring efforts to gather accurate information for the Resource Guides;

- Susanne Terry, Ellen Domski, Jim Dobkowski, Sarah Gowan, Cindy Cook, Daniel Lubetsky, Paul Lambe, and others, for their generous contributions to the stories that enliven and embody the Four Principles of Peace.

ABOUT THE AUTHOR

Louise Diamond has dedicated her life to helping people live in peace, within themselves and with each other. She has had a long career as a professional peacebuilder with individuals, couples, families, communities, organizations, and in places of deep-rooted conflict around the world. She has also worked as a catalyst for healing and the rising tide of peace consciousness in our society.

Louise is the founder and president of The Peace Company, which promotes a culture of peace through products and services that help make peace the way we live. She has written four books and innumerable articles about peace, and is a frequent conference presenter and organizational consultant on related topics.

Louise was also the co-founder, along with Ambassador John McDonald, of the Institute for Multi-Track Diplomacy (IMTD) in Washington, D.C. At IMTD she worked for many years on projects of conflict transformation and peacebuilding in various international settings of ethnic and communal strife.

Louise received her Ph.D. in Peace Studies from the Union Institute in 1990. She lives in the beautiful Green Mountains of Vermont, where she is a Peace Minister of Sunray Meditation Society.

OTHER WORKS BY LOUISE DIAMOND

If you liked this book, you will surely enjoy Louise Diamond's previous work, *The Courage for Peace* (Conari Press, 2000). In that work, she weaves four basic spiritual principles of peace with practical ideas on how to be a peacebuilder in your life and in the world.

Full of inspiring stories from her own journey as a peacebuilder, and from other peacebuilders around the planet, *The Courage for Peace* is a book that will touch your heart, fill you with hope, and remind you that the Spirit of Peace is alive and well in all our lives.

> "Louise Diamond has given us a path that we might follow, a way that we might arrive at the place where we all say that we want to be. . . . Here are practical examples, real-life stories of how real-life people have lived the real truth of how Life is. . . . There is a way to live together in harmony, and in peace."
>
> —From the foreword by Neale Donald Walsch, author of *Conversations with God*

Louise Diamond is also the author, with Ambassador John McDonald, of *Multi-Track Diplomacy: A Systems Approach to Peace* (Kumarian, 3rd ed., 1996). This groundbreaking book lays out, for the first time, how people from all sectors of society are critical to the success of any peace process in places of deeply rooted conflict.

About The Peace Company

Making peace the way we live is our motto at The Peace Company. We believe that the time has come for the human family to step off the war path and onto the peace path, choosing to create for ourselves and our children an enduring culture of peace. The Peace Company exists to help individuals and organizations realize that vision.

We offer products and services to inspire, engage, and inform people of all ages in their quest for a more peaceful world. We aim to make peace popular, practical and profitable (by demonstrating that peace is good business, too).

Our flagship product is *The Peace Book: 108 Simple Ways to Make a More Peaceful World*. Now in two editions (original and this customized *Celebrate Peace* version), this book has over 75,000 copies in circulation through **The Great Peace Give-Away** (see the next page for more information on this unique grassroots initiative). We offer other tools as well for practical peacebuilding—flags and banners; audio and video products; books and mini-libraries; gifts; inner peace aids; resources for children, parents and teachers; cards; posters; and more.

Our educational programs include on-site, on-line, and home-study courses in Peace Leadership, the Fundamentals of Peacebuilding, How to Raise a Peaceful Child in a Violent World, and

Peacebuilding in Everyday Life.

In addition, we custom-design programs for schools, global organizations, and other groups on peace-related issues, such as violence prevention, conflict resolution, managing change, leadership, and diversity.

To learn more about The Peace Company, please visit our website: www.ThePeaceCompany.com, or contact us at:

The Peace Company
54 Maple Street
Bristol, Vermont 05443

Telephone: 1-888-455-5355 (toll-free)
Fax: 802-453-7197
Email: info@thepeacecompany.com

The Story of the
Great Peace Give-Away

Peace is a precious gift that we can give—to ourselves, to those we care about, and to the world.

In 2001, The Peace Company launched The Great Peace Give-Away, encouraging people from all walks of life to give the gift of peace by purchasing boxfuls of *The Peace Book: 108 Simple Ways to Make a More Peaceful World* at a very affordable price and presenting them to family, friends, colleagues, customers, and others as a way of saying, "I offer you this priceless gift of peace. Please pass it on."

And thousands of people have done just that—passed on the gift. Over 75,000 copies of the book are now in circulation, thanks to teachers, mediators, ministers, students, business leaders, nursing home residents, parents, activists, and many, many others who have chosen to express their values through their actions.

Now, with this new customized *Celebrate Peace* edition of *The Peace Book*, even more opportunities to spread the peace message are available. Our goal is to reach at least 3 million people with this book, to foster a critical mass shift from the culture of violence that now pervades our society to a new and viable culture of peace.

We at The Peace Company believe the times call for the boldness of this vision. We invite you to join us in realizing the dream. The spirit of peace that resides in each and every one of us is awakened in both the one who gives and the one who receives the gift of peace. When that spirit of peace lives through our actions, we truly change the world.

For more information on how you can participate in The Great Peace Give-Away, go to our website: www.ThePeaceCompany.com, or call us toll-free at 1-888-455-5355.

Peace grows when you give it away. Come, let us grow a world of peace together.

PEACE X PEACE
CONNECTING WOMEN FOR PEACE

PEACE X PEACE ("peace by peace") is helping create a world where women are central in building sustainable peace. The Internet-based Global Network is at the heart of PEACE X PEACE.

By facilitating direct one-to-one online communication between women-led groups ("Circles") in the United States with their Sister Circles around the world, PEACE X PEACE shifts fear and misunderstanding to trust and collaboration. Women in Sister Circles inform, mentor, and support each other directly, not through media, not through government policies. In the Global Network, "ordinary" women discover their power to help each other to cultivate peace within themselves, their communities, and their cultures.

Sister Circles are matched by affinity of mutual concerns, skills, and needs. Sister Circle members work in all social components necessary for sustainable peace—financial equity, education, inclusive governments, prevention of abuse against women and children, restorative justice, health, truth in media, and freedom of speech. PEACE X PEACE provides the technology and "match-making," plus dialogue facilitators, translators, and supportive monthly and weekly e-publications.

By bridging the divides of cultures, religions, and castes, PEACE X PEACE is at the cusp of a tipping point where, through balanced partnerships, women and men together will transform fear and hostility into actions that build harmonious cultures.

In the context of Celebrate Peace events, PEACE X PEACE presents an experiential workshop—*Connecting Women for Peace.*

Visit **www.peacexpeace.org** for more information about PEACE X PEACE and the Global Network, and to subscribe to e-publications.

Despite the impulses in our world towards separation and destruction, there is another impulse towards wholeness, connectedness, and healing. Women are the most powerful force in the world to bring us to wholeness and healing, to where we experience every moment that we are one family.

—PATRICIA SMITH MELTON
Executive Director, PEACE X PEACE

The moment we make connections—in education, culture, awareness, media—when we use everything we have to realize the feeling that we are one race together on this planet, then we can start to build peace.

—ISABEL ALLENDE
Author, PEACE X PEACE Advisor

Peace and wholeness are about personal healing as much as about healing the world. We can experience healing in healing relationships. In our conversations, healing will take place. It's all the same – peace, healing, home, life. Peace is a circle.

—SUSAN COLLIN MARKS
Peacebuilder, PEACE X PEACE Advisor

Yesterday our Iraqi sister's e-mail described listening to the bulbul songbirds in her yard while she tried to hold on to hope. I can't wait to share her message and my feeling of connectedness with her and all my Iraqi sisters. Women's compassion knows no geographic, generational, or political boundaries. We make and connect circles of compassion. Without compassion, there can be no enduring peace.

—BARBARA THIBEAULT
Member of the Global Network,
connected to a Sister Circle in Iraq

PEACE X PEACE
CONNECTING WOMEN FOR PEACE

Nina Utne

Peace starts with U.

And that means taking a stand. Our owner, Nina Utne, one of the co-founders of CodePink lives her passion for peace daily. Even if it lands her in jail. Which it has.

At **Utne** magazine, we're all about **U**. About being fearless. About bringing **U** stories that are essential. About inspiring inner peace in order to influence world peace.

As one of the nation's few independent magazines, **Utne** covers what matters to **U** in a way that the mainstream can't. Each issue, our editors tap into our extensive network of change-makers, then read 1500 alternative magazines, books, weeklies, newsletters, zines and web sites in order to reprint and write about what's on the leading edge. What's breaking through. Not breaking down.

So if you're seeking peace, you won't find it by reading between the lines of the mainstream press. Go to the source. The truth-teller. The change agent. Read **Utne** and celebrate peace.

SUBSCRIBE NOW!
www.utne.com